TO:

Bethany

FROM:

Don &
Carol S.

100
FAVORITE
BIBLE
VERSES

100 FAVORITE BIBLE VERSES

Lisa Guest

Illustrations by Karla Dornacher

COUNTRYMAN®

A Division of Thomas Nelson Publishers
Since 1798

Published in Nashville, Tennessee, by Thomas Nelson. Thomas Nelson is a registered trademark of HarperCollins Christian Publishing, Inc.

Thomas Nelson titles may be purchased in bulk for educational, business, fundraising, or sales promotional use. For information, please e-mail SpecialMarkets@ ThomasNelson.com.

Unless otherwise indicated, all Scripture quotations are from the New King James Version. © 1982 by Thomas Nelson. Used by permission. All rights reserved.

Scriptures noted KJV are from the King James Version of the Bible.

Scriptures noted NIV are from The Holy Bible, New International Version®. © 1973, 1978, 1984 by International Bible Society. Used by permission of Zondervan Publishing House. All rights reserved.

Scriptures noted NASB are from the New American Standard Bible. © 1960, 1962, 1963, 1968, 1971, 1972, 1973, 1975, 1977, 1995 by the Lockman Foundation. Used by permission.

Scriptures noted NCV are from the New Century Version®. © 2005 by Thomas Nelson. Used by permission. All rights reserved.

Scriptures noted ESV are from the English Standard Version. © 2001 by Crossway Bibles, a division of Good News Publishers.

Scriptures marked NLT are from the Holy Bible, New Living Translation. © 1996. Used by permission of Tyndale House Publishers, Inc., Wheaton, Illinois 60189. All rights reserved.

Designed by Susan Browne.

ISBN: 978-1-4041-9001-6

Printed in China

16 17 18 19 20 TIMS 13 12 11 10 9 8 7

CONTENTS

INTRODUCTION

What is your favorite verse in the Bible? **Simply try-ing** to answer that question is a wonderful exercise in appreciating both the life-giving power of God's Word and the significant role it has played in your life. How can you possibly choose only one verse—or only five, for that matter!

To compile this collection, we sent out a call for people to share the Bible verses they cherished the most. The responses were many, coming from across the country and across the sea. One thing was certain for all who responded—God's Word had touched each of their lives in a way that was inspired and deeply personal. One had written that a passage from the Psalms had spoken words of comfort when she was feeling alone. For another, a parable of Jesus had inspired him to pray as he'd never prayed before.

Scripture truly is living and active (Hebrews 4:12), speaking to us in different ways at different times. God uses His Word to guide us in times of doubt and sustain us in times of loss. His words become a rich tool as we pray Scripture back to its Author, and He enables us to remember specific passages so that we can comfort others and share His life-changing truth. The Bible teaches us not only how to live but also why we live—and it reminds us that God wins in the end.

So what *is* your favorite verse? When you hear that question, your current favorite may come to mind right away. Or your first thought could be a life verse you chose when you named Jesus as your Savior and Lord. Maybe your parents shared a passage with you often as a child, and it has remained in your heart.

Or perhaps life is difficult right now, and you have recently discovered a verse that you know the Lord handpicked just for you for just this time. It is definitely your current favorite. Or maybe a particular verse was that kind of blessing-for-a-season at a different point in your life, and those words will always be incredibly meaningful to you.

In the pages that follow, you'll find some of your own favorite verses, a few that may surprise you, and perhaps a new friend as well. If you'd like, use the final pages to add more favorites to the collection. You'll find that each passage offers its own gifts of comfort, direction, hope, and inspiration.

Enjoy this hold-in-your-hands, tangible reminder of the treasures that await you in God's Word. May this devotional grow your appreciation for Scripture and fuel your passion to read it, know it, and live it.

Finally, may Scripture truly be a light unto the path you walk in this world—and, encouraged by God's Word, may you know rich blessings of joy in Him each step of the way!

PSALM 119:105

Your word is a lamp to my feet
and a light to my path.

SHARE THE
BLESSING OF GOD'S
PERFECT LOVE.

1 CORINTHIANS 13:4–7

Love is patient and kind. Love is not jealous
or boastful or proud or rude. It does not
demand its own way. It is not irritable,
and it keeps no record of being wronged. It
does not rejoice about injustice but rejoices
whenever the truth wins out. Love never gives
up, never loses faith, is always hopeful, and
endures through every circumstance. (NLT)

Maybe you've heard it suggested that you read these verses from 1 Corinthians 13 as a description of Christ. That certainly works. Each statement about love is an accurate description of our Lord, who—acting on His immeasurable love for us—died on the cross for our sins.

Maybe you've heard the suggestion that, as you read them, replace the word *love* with your own name. That can be a very convicting exercise as we realize how far short of God's standards we fall. God is love (1 John 4:8), but we struggle to love. And we often fail.

Here is another option. As you read these words today, think of them as a description of God's love for you, because they are that too. In these quiet moments, let God speak His love to you. Let His love heal you, encourage you, and guide you. Let Him use these words of love to reinforce the truth that nothing will ever separate you from His love (Romans 8:38–39) and that He will never leave you (Matthew 28:20).

After basking in God's love for a while, ask Him whom He would like for you to love today with His love. He may bring to mind someone you need to forgive (love "keeps no record of being wronged"), He may prompt you to pray about tonight's homework sessions with the kids ("love is patient"), or He may nudge you to take brownies to the new neighbors or a meal to a grieving family (love is "kind"). Listen for God's direction, do whatever He says, and enjoy the blessing that comes with obeying Him and loving others with His love.

Thank You, Lord God, that You will never give up on me and You will never lose faith in me. Thank You for the reassurance and hope I find in that truth. Thank You, too, for the privileged calling of being able to love others with Your love. Help me die to myself so that I will hear Your guiding voice—and then help me follow You with joy. God, You are love. Please use me to help others know that.

JOHN 3:16

For God so loved the world, that he gave his only begotten Son, that whosoever believeth in him should not perish, but have everlasting life. (KJV)

MAY WE LIVE AWARE

OF GOD'S GREAT

GIFT OF LIFE.

John 3:16 may be the most widely known and most frequently memorized verse in the Bible. Sadly, our familiarity with these words can make it hard for us to really hear their vital message. Let's try to listen to the words as if for the first time.

"For God so loved the world," and He chose to demonstrate His love with an action that became the focal point of history. God "gave His only begotten Son" to the very people who had turned their backs on Him, who had rejected His ways and were instead satisfied to live as they saw fit. This giving required a sacrifice beyond measure on the part of both God the Father and God the Son. The Son would not only go to the cross, but He would also experience complete separation from His Father.

But after three days, God the Father raised Jesus the Son from the dead, demonstrating His power over sin and death. And "whosoever believeth in [the resurrected Christ] should not perish, but have everlasting life." That life of intimate communion and life-giving fellowship with the Father begins with our declaration of faith and lasts throughout eternity.

Is that verse still too familiar to truly hear? Consider Charles Spurgeon's comments: "My hope lives not because I am not a sinner, but because I am a sinner for whom Christ died; my trust is not that I am holy, but that being unholy, he is my righteousness. My faith rests not upon what I am, or shall be, or feel, or know, but in what Christ is, in what he has done and in what he is now doing for me."[1]

Let's hear an amen!

As the old hymn says, Father God, Your love is so amazing and so divine that it truly does demand my life, my all. May I journey through this day—this life—aware of Your constant presence with me. Keep my eyes focused on Jesus, my heart overflowing with love for You, and my lips ready to share the good news of the gospel.

JOSHUA 1:9

Have I not commanded
you? Be strong and
of good courage; do
not be afraid, nor be
dismayed, for the LORD
your God is with you
wherever you go.

"THE LORD YOUR GOD IS WITH

YOU WHEREVER YOU GO."

Nothing in your life surprises God. Every event, every conversation, every joy, and every sorrow—He has either planned or allowed all these.

Nothing in this world surprises God. He designed the pristine creation that has been ravaged by sin for millennia. He knows the human heart better than we understand ourselves. He knows that life on this planet will mean trials, pain, heartache, and struggle.

God was, for instance, well aware of the challenges that faced Joshua when he obediently stepped up to lead the people of Israel after Moses' death. The Almighty knew that Joshua would have occasion to feel weak, overwhelmed, and discouraged. He also knew that Joshua had very legitimate reasons to fear and be dismayed. And God spoke to those needs—which are your needs as well: "Be strong and of good courage; do not be afraid, nor be dismayed."

But God didn't stop there for Joshua—and He doesn't stop there for you. He gives you an empowering reason why you needn't fear or be discouraged. That reason? "Because the LORD your God is with you wherever you go."

So whatever may make you feel anything but strong and courageous—perhaps the daily news, the state of the international economy, pressures and demands at work, the challenges of raising kids, and undoubtedly a few items you can add to the list—remind yourself that God is with you. And put one foot in front of the other one more time.

Thank You, Lord God, for being with me always, wherever I go. Keep me mindful that You, my Source of strength and encouragement, are at my side every minute of every day. In light of these truths, I have no reason to be afraid or dismayed. So, knowing that I am loved by You, may I live with confidence and joy.

PSALM 23

The Lord is my shepherd;
   I shall not want.
He makes me to lie down in green pastures;
   He leads me beside the still waters.
He restores my soul;
   He leads me in the paths of righteousness
   For His name's sake.
Yea, though I walk through the valley of the shadow
      of death,
   I will fear no evil;
   For You are with me;
   Your rod and Your staff, they comfort me.
You prepare a table before me in the presence of
      my enemies;
   You anoint my head with oil;
   My cup runs over.
Surely goodness and mercy shall follow me
   All the days of my life;
   And I will dwell in the house of the Lord
   Forever.

In his classic *A Shepherd Looks at Psalm 23*, writer Phillip Keller offers many insights into the words of David, the shepherd of days gone by. For instance, are you aware of how similar sheep and human beings are? It's not a pretty picture! "Our mass mind (or mob instincts), our fears and timidity, our stubbornness and stupidity, our perverse habits are all parallels of profound importance," Keller has noted.

Although we might not choose that kind of company, Jesus graciously does, and "He is ever interceding for us; He is ever guiding us by His gracious Spirit; He is ever working on our behalf to ensure that we will benefit from His care. . . . the Good Shepherd spares no pains for the welfare of His sheep."[2]

YOUR GOOD

SHEPHERD

PROVIDES 24/7

CARE FOR YOU.

The cross is the supreme example of Jesus sparing "no pains" for His sheep who were lost in sin. Yet Jesus' shepherding didn't stop on Calvary. Read again the promises in Psalm 23. What provision are you most in need of today? What image offers you peace? What words offer you hope?

Thank your Good Shepherd for His thorough, 24/7 care for you. Ask forgiveness for the ways you fall into step with the world's flock rather than sticking with God's sheep. Then close with praise for the "goodness and mercy" that, by God's grace, will follow you all the days of your life and into eternity.

Lord, with You as my shepherd, I will never lack anything I need. I want to listen to You and follow Your leading to good pastures and clean water. I long for You to restore my soul when I stray. Help me to walk along Your paths of righteousness for my good and Your glory.

1 JOHN 1:9

If we confess our sins, He is faithful and just to forgive us our sins and to cleanse us from all unrighteousness.

YOU ARE FORGIVEN BECAUSE OF JESUS' ACT OF COSTLY LOVE AT CALVARY.

I knew, because of my own feelings, there was something wrong with me, and I knew it wasn't only me. I knew it was everybody. It was like a bacteria or a cancer or a trance. It wasn't on the skin; it was in the soul. . . . It was as if we were cracked, couldn't love right, couldn't feel good things for very long without screwing it all up."[3] So wrote Donald Miller in *Blue Like Jazz* about his becoming aware of his own sin, of the sin nature that is inherent in all of us.

King David would agree that sin works like bacteria. Speaking about personal experience, he testified that unconfessed sin affects a person's physical health. David knew there was no "health in my bones because of my sin" (Psalm 38:3), and he acknowledged that "my strength fails because of my iniquity, and my bones waste away" (31:10).

The apostle John speaks to both Donald Miller and David with this life-giving truth: when we confess our sins, God forgives us—and His forgiveness is not some cold, businesslike transaction. After all, it was made possible by an act of immeasurable and costly love. Our God let His sinless Son die on the cross as payment for Donald Miller's sin, David's sin, and your sin. This payment for sin made possible a cleansing: God removes our sins from us as far as the east is from the west (Psalm 103:12), and He washes us whiter than snow (51:7).

Yes, there's something wrong with us: we are sinners. But on the cross at Calvary, our Savior paid the price for us, and now our holy God graciously forgives us and cleanses us.

Jesus taught that the truth shall set us free, and the truth about my sin and about Your gracious forgiveness, Father God, has done just that—set me free! Thank You that I don't have to pretend my sin isn't there and that I don't have to suffer as David did. Thank You that I don't have to perform to earn Your forgiveness, but that Your Son paid the price for me. Thank You for this amazing truth about Your amazing grace.

MICAH 6:8

He has shown you, O man, what is good;
And what does the Lord require of you
But to do justly,
To love mercy,
And to walk humbly with your God?

GOD HAS SHOWN US HOW
TO LIVE A LIFE THAT
GLORIFIES HIM.

Ow do you make a peanut butter sandwich? Put the peanut butter on the bread. Oh, well, yes, of course you open the bag of bread and take out two pieces. Then you unscrew the lid from the peanut butter jar and, using a knife, spread some peanut butter on one of the slices of bread.

Showing, not merely telling, is a much more effective way of teaching. And God has shown us what is good. Think about David keeping his promise to Jonathan and caring for Mephibosheth (2 Samuel 9): David did justly. Abraham prayed fervently, asking God to spare the city of Sodom if there were fifty righteous people and, finally, if there were only ten (Genesis 18:16–33). God loves mercy. And Esther acted boldly "for such a time as this" (Esther 4:14). She walked humbly with God.

God's most powerful illustration of what is good, however, is His own Son. Jesus overturned the tables of the money changers who had made His Father's house a den of thieves. He paid taxes—with money he got from a fish's mouth. And He spoke out openly against the hypocrisy of Jewish church leaders who used their power for their own good. Jesus did justly.

Jesus healed the sick, made the blind see, and enabled the lame to walk. He freed people from demons and illness. He reached out to Samaritans, prostitutes, and tax collectors, to sinners like you and me. Jesus loved mercy.

Jesus submitted to God's will to the point of dying on a cross. After His agonizing prayers in Gethsemane, Jesus ultimately agreed to do the Father's will, not His own. Jesus walked humbly with His God. May we walk in our Savior's footprints.

I do learn better, Father, when someone shows me something rather than just tells me about it. So I thank You for showing me in many people of the Bible—and especially in Jesus Himself—what is good. By Your Spirit, may I learn to do justly, to love mercy, and to walk humbly with You. Today and always.

LUKE 10:27

"You shall love the LORD your God with all your heart, with all your soul, with all your strength, and with all your mind" and "your neighbor as yourself."

GOD'S LOVE CAN FREE US TO LOVE IN RETURN.

When Jesus was asked what a person needs to do to inherit eternal life, His response was to love God with all you are and love your neighbor just as you love yourself. These commands are straightforward and simple enough to understand. Living them out, however, is an entirely different matter—and the second command is especially difficult if you don't find it easy to love yourself.

In *Take Your Best Shot: Do Something Bigger Than Yourself*, Austin Gutwein comments on the fact that loving ourselves can be tough. Why? He suggests that we tend to look at externals, many of which are based in the world's ideas of loveable. But God is more concerned about the internals, not about how we look or what we do. In Austin's words, "God doesn't look at us the way we do. . . . When we can begin to see ourselves the way God sees us, we may find it easier to love ourselves."

So spend time reading God's Word. It's been called His love letter to humanity! Spend time listening for His whispered words of love to you and the firm impressions on your heart that happen in the quiet moments you spend with Him. Finally, keep your eyes open for evidence of His faithfulness to you. His actions on your behalf and in answer to your prayers do indeed speak volumes about His love for you.

So go ahead and believe this: "God is crazy about you. And he needs you to love yourself so you can go out and show his love to others."[4]

You know my heart, Lord. You know the ways I struggle to love and even to accept myself. You also know how difficult it can be for me to love others, and we both know I totally fail at loving You with all I am. Yet I choose to believe what Your Word teaches: that You love me and that nothing can separate me from that love. May Your love transform me and free me to love myself, to love others better, and to love You with more of myself.

RUTH 1:16–17

Entreat me not to leave you,

    Or to turn back from following after you;

    For wherever you go, I will go;

    And wherever you lodge, I will lodge;

    Your people shall be my people,

    And your God, my God.

Where you die, I will die,

    And there will I be buried.

    The LORD do so to me, and more also,

    If anything but death parts you and me.

GOD'S LOYALTY TO YOU

WILL NEVER WAVER, FADE,

OR GATHER DUST.

Loyalty. That word may sound like it needs to be dusted off. As a society, we seem to have relegated it to the Boy Scout laws. Behavior today too often suggests that loyalty is a dated concept, a fading virtue.

Gone are the days when an employee stays with a company for several decades rather than a handful of years. The high divorce rate as well as the declining rate of marriage point to the same change of values. Maybe a fan will cheer on the same team for a lifetime despite the win/loss record (think of those diehard Cubs fans!), but to what else—if anything—are we as loyal?

In today's passage we see Ruth making a shockingly strong statement of loyalty. She declares her loyalty to her mother-in-law, Naomi; her willingness to travel to Naomi's land; and her openness to settling among Naomi's people. The most startling aspect of Naomi's declaration of loyalty, though, is her pledge to follow Naomi's God. Ruth chose to forsake all she had known growing up in Moab; she chose to follow the God of Israel, the true and living God. Like Abraham before her, Ruth left behind her family and her homeland in response to God's call on her life. Ruth declared her loyalty to Him with her words and her actions.

Today you may have opportunities with your words or actions to declare your loyalty to God. Do so, knowing that your faithful and loyal God will guide and empower you. You may waver in your loyalty to Him, but know that His loyalty and faithfulness to you will never waver, fade, or gather dust.

Lord, use me as Your light as I choose to be loyal to my spouse, my friends, my church family, and perhaps even to a company. Most of all, though, may I be loyal to You. May my words and my actions manifest Ruth's declaration: may I be loyal to You, almighty God, unto death!

PSALM 32:8

I will instruct you and teach you
in the way you should go;
I will guide you with My eye.

GOD WILL DIRECT YOU.

TAKE TIME TO LISTEN

FOR HIS VOICE.

Whether you find directions to your intended destination on a high-tech computer or an old-fashioned, hold-in-your-hands-and-try-to-refold-it-later map, the task takes time. Not a lot of time, but some time. We all know, though, that the time we spend seeking directions is probably only a fraction of the time it might take us to get un-lost if we don't seek out directions before we start our journey.

This same principle holds true in life, and it definitely pertains to our spiritual journey. God will give us directions, but we need to take time to listen. We need to make time to read His Word and hear it taught, and when we pray, we need to spend time listening for His voice. According to Sarah Young, the author of *Jesus Calling*, it is as if our Lord is saying, "Trust Me enough to spend ample time with Me, pushing back the demands of the day. . . . Because I am omnipotent, I am able to bend time and events in your favor. You will find that you can accomplish *more* in less time, after you have given yourself to Me in rich communion. Also, as you align yourself with My perspective, you can sort out what is important and what is not."[5]

Do you believe this truth? Perhaps you've lived it and continue to live it, enjoying an intimate relationship with your heavenly Father. Or perhaps you've never believed this truth enough to actually take this kind of faith step. If that's the case, what do you have to lose? Make time with your Lord a priority, watch Him bless the rest of your day, and learn anew that you can take God at His word. God promises to teach you and guide you. Give Him the chance!

Lord God, it's easier to say I have faith in You than it is to take steps of faith. And that confession doesn't surprise You at all! I do want to walk the path You want me to travel. Enable me to take the step of faith involved in making time to listen for Your instructions—and then enable me to travel according to Your directions.

PRAY ABOUT

EVERYTHING

AND EXPERIENCE

GOD'S PEACE.

PHILIPPIANS 4:6–7

Be anxious for nothing, but
in everything by prayer and
supplication, with thanksgiving, let
your requests be made known to
God; and the peace of God, which
surpasses all understanding,
will guard your hearts and
minds through Christ Jesus.

It's a command that comes with a promise. Pray. Pray about everything. Pray all the time. Pray with thanksgiving. The apostle Paul didn't leave loopholes. He didn't identify seasons of life, specific situations, or extenuating circumstances when God's people can take a break from praying. Knowing that worry is our default mode, Paul urged God's people to pray for God's presence with us and for the people He puts in our paths.

GRAMMY Award winner and Dove Award recipient Rebecca St. James also knows the importance of prayer. She urges her audiences, "Never stop praying. Realize the awesome fact that we get to talk to the Creator of the world!"[6]

Rebecca starts every morning by committing the day to the Lord in prayer, and she prays throughout the day, before every event on the schedule. She has seen God answer in amazing ways, and she values the ongoing communication with Him. "We must foster a lifestyle which encourages . . . praying that we'll have Jesus' heart and Jesus' attitude," she explains, "[and be] more God conscious than self-conscious. We need to keep that conversation going."

As if this intimate communication with the Creator of the world weren't reward enough in and of itself, Paul knew that prayer also means trading anxiety for God's peace. The apostle knew much about dangers and reasons to worry, but he practiced what he preached. He prayed and knew unshakable, incomprehensible, divine peace. You can know it too. Don't worry, pray about everything, and experience God's peace.

Prayer is an amazing privilege, Lord, yet too often I take it for granted. Forgive me, and fuel in me a desire to establish and maintain an ongoing conversation with You. I do want to learn to pray always and about everything and to do so with thanksgiving. Please teach me, so that each day I will see You more clearly, love You more dearly, and follow You more nearly.

ISAIAH 40:28–31

Have you not known?

Have you not heard?

The everlasting God, the LORD,

The Creator of the ends of the earth,

Neither faints nor is weary.

His understanding is unsearchable.

He gives power to the weak,

And to those who have no might He increases strength.

Even the youths shall faint and be weary,

And the young men shall utterly fall,

But those who wait on the LORD

Shall renew their strength;

They shall mount up with wings like eagles,

They shall run and not be weary,

They shall walk and not faint.

THE LORD WILL

BE THE WIND

BENEATH YOUR

WEARY WINGS.

Some facts about eagles for you today . . .

Eagles have a seven-foot wingspan, and they are able to carry well over their body weight. Their strength is also evident when they appear to be motionless in hurricane-force winds. Eagles can reach speeds of more than one hundred fifty miles per hour and dive at the speed of two hundred miles per hour. These amazing birds can soar half a mile above the earth and glide at altitudes of more than 2,500 feet. And as eagles perform these amazing feats, they appear to do so effortlessly.[7]

With these facts in mind, consider again the promise in Isaiah that you "shall mount up with wings like eagles." Yes, you will grow weary—physically, emotionally, mentally, and spiritually—as you journey through life, but you don't have to stay at that low point. Turn to God; wait on Him. Open His Word and remind yourself of His strength, power, and love. Find time to worship Him. Think back over God's great faithfulness to you. Kneel and pray. Let God know what He already knows, that you are feeling overwhelmed, vulnerable, weak, and nearly at a breaking point. Let Him lift you up.

One more eagle fact. The eagle's feathers are replaced each year. In contrast to some birds, though, the eagle is never left incapacitated during molting. Similarly, as you wait upon the Lord, you will find yourself replenished and refreshed. You will never find yourself incapacitated because the Lord will be the wind beneath your wings. As you rest in His strength, you will find your hopelessness replaced by hope; your weariness by energy; and your fear by courage.

Creator God, You know I am made from dust; You know that I do grow tired and weary. I thank You for inviting me to draw near to You when I am in need of the kind of refreshment and renewal only You can give. Fill me when I'm empty, I pray, with strength, hope, and joy rooted in You.

HEBREWS 4:12

The word of God is living
and active, sharper than
any two-edged sword,
piercing to the division
of soul and of spirit, of
joints and of marrow,
and discerning the
thoughts and intentions
of the heart. (ESV)

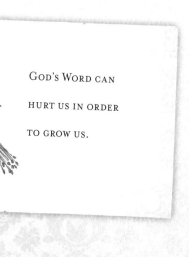

GOD'S WORD CAN

HURT US IN ORDER

TO GROW US.

Something that hurts us can actually be good for us. Getting a flu shot, setting a broken bone, hearing the truth about where we are messing up our walk with the Lord—hurts like these are, in the long run, good for us.

God's Word is that kind of tool if we let it be: it can hurt us in order to heal us and grow us. Understanding that, the author of Hebrews described Scripture as "living and active, sharper than any two-edged sword." He was aware that, as it pierces our hearts, God's Word reveals the sinful thoughts, motives, and desires that reside there.

In *Dug Down Deep*, Joshua Harris put it this way: "When we read it, the Bible opens *us* up. It reads us. It searches us in the deepest way possible. It reveals our hearts and motivations. It convicts and comforts us."[8]

Think about when you have felt the Bible pierce your heart. When has God's Word provided comfort and peace beyond understanding? When did God use Scripture to guide you or help you make a decision? And when did God's Word convict you of your sin and help you recognize the thoughts and attitudes that do not please Him?

Yes, God's Word reveals to us our sin, and that's never a pretty picture. But seeing our sin for what it is is key to confessing it, receiving forgiveness for it, and being delivered from its hold on us. God has designed His living and active Word to be exactly what we need. This truth-revealing tool is invaluable to our growth toward Christlikeness.

Thank You for this reminder of the power of Your Word. With the Bible so readily available, it's easy to get numb to the heart surgery and life change that Scripture can work in me when I read it. Teach me, Lord, to read Your Word with a heart that is open to Your transforming work and willing to be hurt by Your truth in order to become more like Your Son.

LUKE 1:37

For with God nothing
will be impossible.

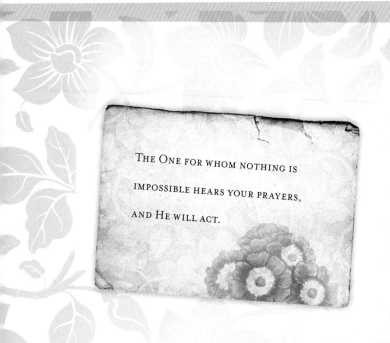

THE ONE FOR WHOM NOTHING IS
IMPOSSIBLE HEARS YOUR PRAYERS,
AND HE WILL ACT.

We are used to hearing promises that are too good to be true. But we aren't at all used to promises being delivered by an angel of the Lord. Neither was Mary.

This young girl was going about her daily duties when suddenly the angel Gabriel came calling. As if his appearance weren't surprising enough, his announcement made his remarkable presence pale in comparison. *She* was favored by the Lord? *She* was blessed among women? She, who had never been with a man, would conceive a son? And what was this talk about thrones and kingdoms and forever? And had Gabriel really said to call this miracle baby "the Son of God"?

The answer to these questions was yes, and Gabriel sealed his announcement with this black-and-white, matter-of-fact statement: "With God nothing will be impossible." In case Mary was a bit skeptical (certainly an understandable reaction!), the angel reported that her relative Elizabeth, childless and advanced in years, was six months pregnant. Maybe all Gabriel said was true. Maybe nothing is impossible for God.

What situation in your life seems impossible? What physical circumstances, what state of the heart, what relationship seems beyond repair and even beyond hope? Do you need to find a job? Have you been praying that someone you love will once again walk with the Lord? Are you asking the Lord to renew the passion in your marriage?

Keep calling out to the One for whom nothing is impossible, the powerful God of redemption, the loving God who calls you His child. He hears, and He will act.

I cry out to You, the God of the impossible, and ask You to work in those impossible situations in my life. You who are all wise, all loving, and all powerful can change circumstances, hearts, and relationships. You know the impossibilities I'm concerned about, and I ask You to intervene—for the good of those involved and for Your glory.

MATTHEW 6:19–21

Do not lay up for yourselves
treasures on earth, where moth
and rust destroy and where
thieves break in and steal; but
lay up for yourselves treasures
in heaven, where neither moth
nor rust destroys and where
thieves do not break in and
steal. For where your treasure is,
there your heart will be also.

LEARN TO VALUE
WHAT GOD VALUES.

It's always easier to see other people's shortcomings than our own. We can readily identify, say, the person who is clawing up the ladder of success and pursuing the latest technology, the biggest Lexus, the finest gated community, and the most elite schools for the children.

But maybe we're not so different. Perhaps our love for earthly stuff is simply less obvious because we're in a different income bracket or at a different season of life. So be honest. What stuff are you holding on to with a death grip? And what stuff are you able to hold loosely, recognizing it as a gift from God and knowing that He has asked you to be a good steward of it?

Spend some time thinking about these wise words from Angela Thomas's book *A Beautiful Offering*: "Laying up treasure in heaven is about learning to value what is valuable to God. It will probably mean coming to appreciate the intangible riches of the kingdom inheritance more than the visible accumulation of stuff on earth. It might mean that . . . mercy gets a better rating than mutual funds and sacrifice appraises higher than self."

More specifics? Angela obliges: "Things like serving the church, sacrificing my time or my comfort for the needs of others. . . . People matter to God and hearts matter to God and love matters more than anything."[9] She also lists these credits to your heavenly account: forgiveness given, grace extended, warm hugs, tender looks, heartfelt contentment, joy, and love.

How healthy is your heavenly bank account? And when will you make your next deposit?

Father God, teach me to value what is valuable to You. Along those lines, please sharpen in me a sensitivity to hurting people so that I might come alongside them. Help me hear You and obey when You call me to serve. Enable me to forgive as I've been forgiven and to extend to others the kind of grace You have extended to me. Help me not miss opportunities to lay up treasures in heaven.

GOD CREATED COUNTLESS SOMETHINGS OUT OF NOTHING.

GENESIS 1:3

Then God said, "Let there be light"; and there was light.

When we create, we use what has already been created. We go to the pantry for the flour, sugar, salt, baking powder, and cocoa powder. Our chocolate cake is then on its way to being a reality.

When God began creating everything that exists, He didn't have a pantry to go to. He created something—countless somethings—out of nothing. He didn't have atoms, molecules, cells, or DNA to choose from and mix up and bake for thirty to forty minutes. He didn't have a tried-and-true recipe to follow. He was on His own—and the absolutely amazing creation that we know was the result. From microscopic organisms like dust mites to the surging oceans that make up 70 percent of Planet Earth, from fluorescent sea life glowing in the depths of the sea to eagles soaring above the mountain heights, from relatively simple minerals to the wondrously complex human body—God Almighty did it all Himself.

The first step in God's creative process was the creation of light. According to Genesis, "In the beginning God created the heavens and the earth. The earth was without form, and void; and darkness was on the face of the deep (1:1–2). Then God commanded, "Let there be light," and it was so.

Truly, nothing is impossible for God—and what a comforting truth. He made out of nothing this universe we live in. He can make something of the nothing that you may feel your life has become. Submit to Him as did the "darkness . . . on the face of the deep," and see what our powerful and creative God does.

"Let there be light." Lord God, how those four words speak volumes about Your infinite power and Your absolute sovereignty! I find real comfort and hope in the fact that You are all powerful and totally in control of the universe, of the world's history, and of my journey through life. May those four words keep me mindful that nothing is impossible for You as I face situations that seem impossible to me.

PSALM 118:5

I called on the LORD in distress;
The LORD answered me and
set me in a broad place.

OUR FAITHFUL
GOD ANSWERS
OUR CALLS.

Oh, give thanks to the Lord, for He is good! For His mercy endures forever." This joyful note opens Psalm 118, and the joy continues as the psalmist celebrates God's faithfulness to him through the years.

Now consider God's great faithfulness to you through the years. Think first about your own salvation story and how God brought you to the point of naming Jesus as Savior and Lord.

Following the psalmist's path through Psalm 118, think about times of distress you have experienced, times you felt crowded in and suffocated, when you longed to have the Lord deliver you. When have you called on the Lord in such a time of distress and experienced His taking you to "a broad place" where you could breathe deeply and feel safe (verse 5)?

Recall a time when you could have trusted in something the world offered, but you took a step of faith and trusted the Lord instead (verses 8–9). When have you been surrounded by the nations, figuratively speaking, and unquestionably experienced God's deliverance (verses 10–14)? Overflowing with gratitude, the psalmist vowed to "declare the works of the Lord" (verse 17). In what ways are you doing so in your life? When has the Lord "chastened [you] severely" (verse 18), and what good did God bring out of that experience?

Near the end of the song, the psalmist proclaimed, "You are my God, and I will praise You; You are my God, I will exalt You" (verse 28). The joyous tone is unmistakable—and may that joy in the Lord and gratitude to Him be unmistakable in our words, our attitudes, and our actions.

Lord, You are good! You are faithful! You have delivered me from difficult circumstances and helped me learn from them. May I always be conscious of these reasons for joy and may my life reflect my gratitude to You. Just as the joyous tone of Psalm 118 is unmistakable, may joy in You be unmistakable in my life.

JAMES 5:16

The effective, fervent prayer of a righteous man avails much.

BY GOD'S GRACE, OUR

PRAYERS CAN AND

WILL AVAIL MUCH.

The power of prayer is one of the mysteries of our faith. We go through dry seasons when God seems distant and prayer seems pointless, so we skip it altogether. We may feel discouraged from praying for a specific person or situation for months, if not years or decades. We may also enter a season of great pain and loss when we simply can't pray, and we rely on the faithful and faith-full prayers of our sisters and brothers in Christ.

Then come those prayer times when God seems to be in the same room with us as we pray, and those seasons of prayer when God responds in ways far greater than we dared ask or would have ever imagined. We enter our times of prayer with great anticipation that God will work mightily—in situations and in our hearts—as a result of our time with Him.

In between these two extreme experiences are those regular prayer times, those acts of disciplined obedience that we do out of love for our Lord. We pray because He calls us to; we pray because we love Him.

James reminds us that, by God's grace, our prayers can and will avail much. God has declared us righteous, cleansed of our sin by the blood of His Son. We are privileged to be adopted into God's family, and as His children we have the 24/7 opportunity to talk with Him. So may we just do it!

After all, as pastor David Jeremiah points out, "The surest way not to get an answer to prayer is not to pray!"[10]

Thank You for the privilege of prayer, and forgive me when I take for granted the awesome truth that I am able to speak to You, the sovereign King, the Creator of all, the Healer of my soul, anytime and from anywhere. I am grateful for those seasons of prayer when You answer quickly and obviously, and I am grateful that You understand those dry times I go through. So, Father God, please keep me disciplined and expectant as I pray.

WHEN WE ARE
AWARE OF OUR
WEAKNESSES, WE
RELY MORE ON GOD.

2 CORINTHIANS 12:8–10

Three times I pleaded with the Lord to take
[a thorn in my flesh, a messenger of Satan]
away from me. But he said to me, "My grace is
sufficient for you, for my power is made perfect
in weakness." Therefore I will boast all the more
gladly about my weaknesses, so that Christ's
power may rest on me. That is why, for Christ's
sake, I delight in weaknesses, in insults, in
hardships, in persecutions, in difficulties. For
when I am weak, then I am strong. (NIV)

No one knows what this thorn in Paul's flesh was, and that missing piece of information was undoubtedly intentional. After all, the truth that Paul learned and wanted to teach us is now relevant to everyone. Whatever that affliction actually was simply does not matter. The truth God had taught Paul—and that Paul then taught us—matters greatly.

And what was that truth? The apostle had learned that Jesus' grace was all he needed, whatever life's demands. The risen Lord Himself had told Paul, "My grace is sufficient for you, for my power is made perfect in weakness." Paul, therefore, wanted to boast about his weaknesses and explain to the Corinthians then, and to believers since then, why he delighted in them. Christ's power clearly rested on Paul in his weakness and enabled him to do what he wouldn't have been able to do on his own.

Paul had learned a related lesson on his missionary journeys. He had experienced God faithfully giving him strength when he was weak, insulted, persecuted, and struggling. Again, Paul explained that he could find delight in those tough days: "When I am weak, then I am strong."

When we are aware of our weaknesses, of our need for Jesus, we yield ourselves more fully to God. We give Him room to move in and room to work. And He works not only in circumstances but also in our hearts. May we then, as Paul himself did, find delight in those weaknesses that help us know more fully God's great strength at work in us and through us.

The risen Lord said, "My grace is sufficient for you." Paul said, "When I am weak, then I am strong." And I say thank You for being this kind of loving and personal God. You know my weaknesses, You know the hardships and difficulties I'm dealing with, and You provide me with Your strength for those tough times.

ROMANS 8:1

There is now no condemnation for those who are in Christ Jesus. (NIV)

YOU ARE FORGIVEN

AND CLEANSED,

FOREVER

FREE FROM

CONDEMNATION.

We look for the fine print, alert for exceptions and exclusions. We don't trust that insurance policies will help when we need them, that warranties will still be in effect when the appliance breaks, or that we can indeed be free of our holy God's condemnation for past words, deeds, attitudes, mistakes, and sins.

We may be right not to put all of our faith in a manufacturer's guarantee or a politician's promise. However, we have no need to doubt the freedom from condemnation that Jesus Himself, God's perfect Lamb, grants us.

All of us have sinned; all of us have fallen short of God's standards for us (Romans 3:23). We deserve punishment, which in this case is death for our sins. But the good gospel news is that Jesus took that punishment for us and we are forgiven. Paul, who once called himself the chief of sinners (1 Timothy 1:15), wholeheartedly embraced God's grace and encouraged others to do the same. Hear the confidence in this statement: "There is now no condemnation for those who are in Christ Jesus." No condemnation. Absolutely none.

That glorious truth is underscored by the words of Max Lucado: "You are saved, not because of what you do, but because of what Christ did. And you are special, not because of what you do, but because of whose you are. And you are his."[11]

As God's chosen one, you are forgiven and cleansed, forever free from condemnation, and free to live in God's grace and love, now and for eternity.

Lord, You know those past sins—confessed and forgiven—that still haunt me. And, Lord, You know how I sometimes struggle to accept Your undeserved and unconditional love and forgiveness. Keep me growing in my knowledge of You so that I will be able to receive Your love, rest in Your forgiveness, and live in the freedom of Your unfailing grace now and forever.

FAITH GROWS DURING
QUIET COMMUNION
WITH GOD.

PSALM 46:10

Be still, and
know that
I am God.

Psalm 46:10 is a call that runs counter to our culture. But it seems to have run against human expectations for thousands of years.

Consider the prophet Elijah. He boldly stood before the evil King Ahab and proclaimed a God-ordained drought (1 Kings 17:1). Elijah prayed for food for the widow and her son. He revived the boy when he got sick and died. Facing Ahab a second time and accusing him of forsaking the Lord's commandments (18:18), Elijah challenged the prophets of Baal to a contest. After God won that dramatic showdown, Queen Jezebel wanted Elijah killed. God protected and provided for the prophet when he ran for his life. Alone and with a price on his head, the discouraged Elijah wondered why there was no better reward for his faithful service. In response, God sent rock-breaking wind, an earthquake, a fire, and "after the fire a still small voice" (19:12).

God is able to call forth powerful winds, part a sea, and ravage a nation with plagues. Yet He calls us to know Him not in the spectacular and loud, not in the dramatic and powerful. He calls us to be still. We are to find quiet—internal as well as external—if we are truly to know that He is God. Faith grows during our quiet communion with Him. We may be dazzled by amazing demonstrations of His power, but both believers and nonbelievers too easily forget and demand another miracle.

That God wants to draw near to us, that He wants to communicate with us, that we can hear His still, small voice—aren't these miracle enough? Be still . . . and know that He is God.

Lord, I'm not sure I know how to "be still." My responsibilities are demanding, and things on my "to do" list are always shouting at me. Not that it would be easy, but quieting those externals would be easier than trying to quiet myself internally. My mind races, myriad details call for attention—my head is a noisy place! Please teach me to find quiet, to make quiet, so that I can know You better.

EPHESIANS 1:17–19

[I pray] that the God of our Lord Jesus Christ,
the Father of glory, may give to you the spirit
of wisdom and revelation in the knowledge of
Him, the eyes of your understanding being
enlightened; that you may know what is the
hope of His calling, what are the riches of
the glory of His inheritance in the saints,
and what is the exceeding greatness of
His power toward us who believe.

WHEN YOU PRAY,
ASK GOD TO BE
INVOLVED MORE
IN HEARTS THAN
CIRCUMSTANCES.

I'll pray for you." That's often our response when we hear about someone's hard times. And praying for that person—inviting the all-knowing, all-powerful, all-loving God to work in those specific circumstances—is definitely the right thing to do. But when we pray, maybe we should ask God to touch hearts as well as circumstances.

We can learn from the way the apostle Paul prayed for the believers in Ephesus. He could have undoubtedly prayed for specific needs. But we see that Paul's prayers focused on their hearts.

Paul asked God to give those believers living in Ephesus greater wisdom, knowledge, and understanding of Him and of the values, purpose, and work of His kingdom. The apostle asked God to make hope very real to the Ephesians, to keep them focused on the glorious inheritance of eternal life that awaited them, and to keep them mindful of His great power. After all, that power had raised Jesus from the dead, so it was certainly strong enough to tackle any situation the Ephesians were facing, individually or collectively.

God invites us to pray about anything and everything we are concerned about. We are definitely free to mention the details. But as we pray for specific situations, let us also ask God to bless the people involved with wisdom, knowledge, a God-focus, and a mindfulness of His great power.

Lord, I know You invite me to pray about anything and that no concern is too small or unimportant to You. Yet I don't want to get bogged down in the details and not be praying for the character of those people I care about. So, Lord, right now, I ask You to grant them greater wisdom and a clearer understanding of You and Your kingdom work. I ask You to keep these precious people focused on You and mindful of Your great power.

ISAIAH 40:11

He will feed His flock
like a shepherd;
He will gather the
lambs with His arm,
And carry them in His bosom,
And gently lead those
who are with young.

WHEN YOU'RE HURTING, LET YOUR

HEAVENLY FATHER GATHER YOU

INTO HIS ARMS.

Depending on a person's build, there's a distance of about ten inches between our brains and our hearts. That distance might as well be ten thousand miles sometimes.

We can know a lot of theology. We can stand at the foot of the cross with the writers of the Gospels and see how Jesus fulfilled the Old Testament prophecies about the coming Messiah. We can point to passages that describe His power and His mercy. We can quote scriptures about God's love.

But are we able to feel God's love in our hearts? Do we believe in our hearts that God truly is all powerful and ever merciful? And do we stand at the foot of the cross, knowing in our hearts that Jesus died because of His immeasurable and even inconceivable love for sinners like us? Does our faith extend from biblical knowledge of the head to experiential knowledge of the heart?

Building a bridge between head and heart is especially difficult when we're suffering. Joni Eareckson Tada knows about suffering. Having experienced a paralyzing neck injury when she was a teenager and more recently battling cancer, Joni has some hard-earned wisdom to offer us: "When a person is sorely suffering . . . people are like hurting children looking up into the faces of their parents, crying and asking, 'Daddy, why?' Those children don't want explanations, answers, or 'reasons why'; they want their daddy to pick them up, pat them on the backs, and reassure them that everything is going to be okay."

Isaiah testified to the fact that God will indeed gather us into His arms. So does Joni: "God, like a father, doesn't just give advice. He gives himself."[12]

Lord God, thank You for the encouragement, comfort, and truth of Your written Word. Scripture has guided my steps and nourished my relationship with You. But sometimes words are not enough, so I thank You for Your love and presence with me. Thank You for giving Yourself when I need comfort that words can't communicate.

PHILIPPIANS 4:4

Rejoice in the Lord always. Again I will say, rejoice!

WHATEVER YOUR CIRCUMSTANCES, YOU CAN FIND IN THE LORD REASONS TO REJOICE.

How many red lights did you get on the way home today? Did other lines at the grocery store or gas station move more quickly than yours? Did other people's dogs behave better at the bark park than yours?

It's human nature to notice the red lights, the lines that are moving faster than yours, and the dogs that behave better than yours. This tendency doesn't make it easy to find joy in the day-to-day aspects of life. It instead keeps us focused on ourselves and on how unfair life can be.

But we don't have to live like that. We can learn to obey the command of Philippians 4:4. We can learn to rejoice—always! Note that Paul didn't say to rejoice about your *circumstances*. He didn't call us to celebrate hurtful relationships or painful losses. Speaking on God's behalf, Paul instead commanded us to rejoice in the Lord—in His sovereign power, His unwavering goodness, and His unfailing love. When, despite all that is going on in life, we find in Him reasons to rejoice—and there are plenty—we will know His blessing of hope and peace.

So train yourself to look for evidence of God's presence and activity in your life. Some people call it a "God Hunt"; others play "I Spy." At the dinner table or during their weekly small-group meeting, they let people know when they were very aware of God being at work in their lives.

Be warned! These seeds of joy that you sow will bear the fruit of more joy!

Teach me to rejoice—always! And the key, Lord God, will be to look at You always. Reading Your Word, being with Your people, spending time in prayer, listening for Your voice, looking for evidence of Your work in my life will all reveal reasons to praise You and rejoice in You. May knowing You and coming to know You better bring joy that satisfies and truly eclipses the hurts and challenges of life.

JAMES 1:2–5

My brethren, count it all joy
when you fall into various trials,
knowing that the testing of
your faith produces patience.
But let patience have its perfect
work, that you may be perfect
and complete, lacking nothing.
If any of you lacks wisdom, let
him ask of God, who gives to all
liberally and without reproach,
and it will be given to him.

"Count it all joy"? That sounds like an impossible assignment when the *it* refers to "various trials," doesn't it? Think about the current trials in your life. What is making it tough for you to "count it all joy"? Pain? Fear? The unknown? Frustration? Hard work? The need for healing? Something else?

Yes, "count it all joy" is a tough assignment. It was for first-century Christ-followers just as it is for us today. Those early believers were persecuted for their faith. They knew what it was to suffer because they loved Jesus. But James clearly reminded them—and he reminds us—that God is very aware of those trials and very present in them. God allows trials to test and strengthen your faith in Him and to grow in you greater patience for life's tough times.

Of course those growth pains hurt, yet God enables us to count these tough times "all joy." He has, for instance, graciously revealed Himself to be faithful, wise, and loving. Also, we know from His Word that He can and does redeem the most difficult life experiences. We also know the ultimate security: we will spend eternity with Him who sent His Son to die on the cross for our sins. Yes, the world brings loss, pain, and sorrow, but the promise of eternity can help us remember that there's more to life than what this world has for us.

So, for reasons like these, choose to rejoice not *for* life's trials, but in and *despite* those trials. After all, God is with you on the journey, He will not let you go, and He has reserved a place for you in heaven for eternity.

Lord God, thank You for reminding me that this world is not my home, that both the pain and the joy I experience here are transitory, and that You are sovereign over every day of my life. Having You walk this journey of life with me—that is definitely a reason to rejoice whatever the circumstances of my life.

ISAIAH 55:8–9

"For My thoughts are not
　your thoughts,
　Nor are your ways My ways,"
　says the Lord.
"For as the heavens are higher
　than the earth,
　So are My ways higher than
　your ways,
　And My thoughts than
　your thoughts."

God's ways are
higher, and His ways
are good. Always.

Tornados uproot houses, and earthquakes crumble buildings. Hurricanes flood acres of land, and tsunamis wipe towns off the map. Babies die in their cribs, older folks are ravaged by Alzheimer's, and cancer takes victims of all ages. Families, marriages, and hearts are broken. Any one of these facts of life—and there are many others—are reasons people give for not believing in God. Who wants anything to do with a God who allows such pain and loss?

These realities make even believers scratch their heads. Oh, we know that Jesus warns that we'll have trials and tribulations in this world—but why do children have to suffer because of someone else's sin? And why are devoted Christians among the dead when a natural disaster strikes?

We don't understand God. Why does He heal one person but not another? Why does He allow this tsunami to come to shore but let that hurricane blow itself out over the ocean? We don't understand God, neither did Isaiah thousands of years ago, and neither does Sheila Walsh: "I don't always understand why God works as He does . . . but I do believe He is good all the time. . . . Sometimes He delivers us from a situation . . . sometimes He calls us to walk with a limp, following the One who was wounded for us." But she doesn't stop there. Hear her call to active faith: "I encourage you to invite Christ into the midst of your struggles and heartache. Offer your scars to the One who is scarred for you. The very wounds that seemed that they might break you will be used by God to strengthen you."[13]

Wrestling with the kinds of questions in today's devotional definitely keeps me from reducing You to a number of logical propositions and putting You in a box. Your ways aren't my ways; Your thoughts are beyond my ability to understand. Yet Your Word is clear: You are good. Always. I believe; help my unbelief when life is painful and hard.

JESUS IS

PREPARING A

PLACE FOR YOU

IN ETERNITY.

JOHN 14:1-3

Let not your heart be troubled; you believe in God, believe also in Me. In My Father's house are many mansions; if it were not so, I would have told you. I go to prepare a place for you. And if I go and prepare a place for you, I will come again and receive you to Myself; that where I am, there you may be also.

esus had washed His disciples' feet. *Puzzling. Humiliating!* Jesus had predicted His betrayal and, as He dipped bread with Judas Iscariot, identified the betrayer. *Shocking! Infuriating!* Now Jesus had just told His disciples that He would not be with them much longer. *What?!? Why?!?*

Good-hearted and impulsive as always, Peter immediately proclaimed that he wanted to follow Jesus wherever He was going. Peter even vowed to lay down his life for his Lord. Jesus simply responded with the statement that Peter would deny even knowing Him before the rooster crowed. The mood at the Last Supper grew even more somber.

Jesus knew that His disciples, not totally understanding His words right now, would understand them soon enough and need hope. He knows that you need hope too, the kind of glorious hope that makes the earth's darkness less heavy and oppressive. "I go to prepare a place for you" is that glorious, hope-filled promise that can help you put one foot in front of the other when the darkness is almost tangible.

What is troubling your heart right now? What does it mean that Jesus has gone before you to prepare a place for you in eternity? And what does it mean that you will be with Him? May the answers to these last two questions help you with what you shared in response to the first.

Jesus is not One who just says things to hear Himself talk, fill the silence, or make someone feel better. Your mansion awaits!

Jesus, You turned to God in Gethsemane when Your walk to the cross was imminent. Of course You were troubled! That is an understatement! But what comfort to know that You understand feeling troubled, not looking forward to the future, and not wanting to submit to God's will. Thank You for all You did to provide hope for me when I'm feeling troubled, the hope of eternal life with You.

DEUTERONOMY 31:6, 8

Be strong and courageous.
Do not be afraid or
terrified . . . for the LORD
your God goes with you;
he will never leave you nor
forsake you. . . . The LORD
himself goes before you and
will be with you; he will
never leave you nor forsake
you. Do not be afraid; do
not be discouraged. (NIV)

Maybe it's the solid job. Well, as solid as any job can be today. Maybe it's the savings accounts, carefully diversified and monitored. Maybe it's the extended family, always there for you, 24/7. Maybe it's the degrees on the wall or the walls of a house in the "right" zip code. Maybe it's the good health you work hard to maintain. We can get strength from a variety of sources, but only One will be fully reliable.

Moses knew that truth. In fact, Moses knew *Truth* with a capital T: he knew God and therefore knew that God is the only reliable source of strength. Moses had personally encountered God, first in the burning bush when God called him to serve (Exodus 3) and, later, on Mount Sinai when God delivered the Ten Commandments (Exodus 20). Moses had also personally experienced God's faithfulness during the forty-year exodus—the children of Israel never missed a meal thanks to the good Lord's provision (Exodus 16). And Moses had personally witnessed God in all His glory (Exodus 33). So, with total confidence in his Lord, Moses exhorted Joshua and all of Israel to trust not in their own strength but in the strength of their unfailing God.

As you walk with the Lord through your wildernesses, as you meet with God alone as Moses did on Sinai, as you recognize your heavenly Father's faithful provision for you, as you see His glory revealed in answered prayers, you, too, will know with certainty that God "will never leave you nor forsake you. Do not be afraid; do not be discouraged."

It's easy to see how others trust in false gods and unreliable sources of strength. Please show me, Lord, ways that I am trusting in such false sources of strength or in my own strength instead of in Your strength. Help me see where I am doubting Your faithfulness and trying to control certain situations. Finally, please give me the courage I need to take steps of faith in You. I do want to learn to trust more completely in Your unfailing faithfulness to me.

The Lord—your rock,
your salvation, and
your fortress—will
never let you go.

PSALM 62:2

He alone is my rock
and my salvation;
he is my fortress,
I will never be
shaken. (NIV)

The Bible doesn't whitewash human nature or paint a picture of a pain-free world. Life's hurts raise hard questions. Why would God allow certain situations—and why is He slow to provide resolution and relief? Life is difficult, and the Bible doesn't suggest otherwise.

King David was facing difficult times when he penned Psalm 62. Perhaps it was his son Absalom's heartbreaking rebellion, or maybe someone else had betrayed the king. Whatever the circumstances, David chose to focus on God. He reminded himself that God was his rock, a secure foundation for life. The Lord could deliver him from any situation. David knew that when he was attacked, God was his fortress, a safe place to run to for protection from his enemies.

Now consider the last part of this verse. Sounding entirely confident in his God, David proclaims, "I will never be shaken." Nothing would rattle his faith! But the English Standard Version offers a glimpse of David's humanness: "I shall not be greatly shaken." This translation may be more real-life. Acknowledging at least implicitly the reality that events can shake—at least a little bit—the faith of even the most devoted follower, the psalmist vows to "not be *greatly* shaken" (emphasis added). The shaking isn't down to the core of his convictions, and the shaking doesn't last long. After all, the psalmist knows to turn to his Lord, who is his rock, his salvation, his fortress.

In this fallen world, our faith may get shaken, but the Lord will never let us go.

Thank You for David's example, Father God. He never hesitated to cry out to You or to be completely honest about what he was feeling. And, Lord, You know what I'm feeling and where I'm feeling a bit shaken right now. I'm going to do what David did and remind myself that You are my rock, my salvation, and my fortress. I am thankful that You will never let me go.

PHILIPPIANS 2:5-11

Let this mind be in you which was also in Christ
Jesus, who, being in the form of God, did not
consider it robbery to be equal with God, but
made Himself of no reputation, taking the form
of a bondservant, and coming in the likeness of
men. And being found in appearance as a man,
He humbled Himself and became obedient to
the point of death, even the death of the cross.
Therefore God also has highly exalted Him
and given Him the name which is above every
name, that at the name of Jesus every knee
should bow, of those in heaven, and of those
on earth, and of those under the earth, and
that every tongue should confess that Jesus
Christ is Lord, to the glory of God the Father.

Jesus calls us to serve one another, just as He served His disciples at the Last Supper by washing their dusty feet. Jesus calls us to love one another, just as He did when He let Himself be nailed to the cross so that we might be forgiven. Jesus calls us to love God with all that we are, just as He, acting in love, submitted to God's will and died on the cross to satisfy divine justice.

Our attitude should be the same as Jesus had: a willingness to serve and to love. Yes, Jesus commands it, but He also lived it. He asks us to do nothing that He didn't do Himself—and He served and loved to a greater degree than He will ask us to do.

God the Father, pleased with His Son, exalted Jesus "to the highest place and gave him the name that is above every name" (NIV). May we respond similarly by exalting Jesus in our words and our actions. May we freely confess Him to be Savior and Lord by living in a way that glorifies Him and being ready to share the specifics of the gospel with those around us. May we bow to the risen Lord by submitting to His will and making our relationship with Him our top priority.

> WE ARE TO BE WILLING TO SERVE AND LOVE AS JESUS HIMSELF DID.

And consider the closing scene: one day, God promises "every knee should bow, in heaven and on earth and under the earth, and every tongue confess that Jesus Christ is Lord" (NIV). How glorious that time will be—and how wonderful it is that our praise of Jesus as Lord has already begun!

It is an amazing and glorious picture, almighty God, that image of every person on earth bowing before You and confessing that Jesus Christ is Lord! Thank You for calling me to know that truth even now, that I may enjoy Your forgiveness, Your grace, and Your friendship in this life and forever.

2 TIMOTHY 3:16-17

All Scripture is given
by inspiration of God,
and is profitable for
doctrine, for reproof, for
correction, for instruction
in righteousness, that
the man of God
may be complete,
thoroughly equipped
for every good work.

By the power of the Holy Spirit, the
Bible is living and active.

People who don't want to believe the Bible find many (faulty) reasons for not trusting its accuracy. People who do believe the Bible have strong evidence on their side, evidence that supports the reliability of God's Word.

"The quantity of New Testament manuscripts is unparalleled in ancient literature. There are over 5,000 Greek manuscripts, about 8,000 Latin manuscripts, and another 1,000 manuscripts in other languages. . . . In contrast, the typical number of existing manuscript copies for any of the works of the Greek and Latin authors, such as Plato, Aristotle, Caesar, or Tacitus, ranges from 1 to 20."[14]

The Bible is unique for other reasons as well. More than forty authors wrote over a span of 1,500 to 1,800 years in three languages on three continents. On Scripture's pages, readers can find history, biography, letters, parables, prophecies, sermons, and more. Despite this diversity, the Bible is a coherent work, unified in theme and purpose.

Furthermore, this amazing piece of literature is—by the power of the Holy Spirit—living and active (see Hebrews 4:12), as well as "profitable for doctrine, for reproof, for correction, for instruction in righteousness" (2 Timothy 3:16). No wonder God calls us to be *doers* of the Word, not just hearers (see James 1:22).

So where do you go to hear God's truth? And who holds you accountable for living it out? Both the hearing and the accountability are key to healthy Christian living, and both pieces honor and glorify the Lord.

Lord God, help me build my life on the solid foundation of Your Word. I know Scripture will help me stand up against the strong waves of public opinion, the powerful winds of society's values, and the pull of past tradition. May I be a dedicated student of Your Word, always letting You guide me and grow me through its pages.

JOB 1:21

Naked I came from my mother's womb,
And naked shall I return there.
The LORD gave, and the LORD has taken away;
Blessed be the name of the LORD.

GOD IS

FAITHFUL,

EVEN IN TIMES

OF LOSS.

What two or three concerns are weighing most heavily on your heart right now? Maybe you just learned that Laura's cancer has returned—for the eighth time. Or your college senior is dealing with the consequences of a poor moral decision. Perhaps your eighty-three-year-old mother is not pleased that you are taking away her driver's license. And what, if anything, can you do to help your daughter shake her depression?

Of course all these situations—and those you are concerned about—call for prayer. We fall at the Lord's feet, not necessarily understanding what He's doing, why He has allowed what He has allowed, or why He seems so distant and uncaring. We pray as best we can, and we let others pray for us. We just keep putting one foot in front of the other.

"We're called to be faithful to God even when it seems he hasn't been faithful to us. We're called to love him even when we feel abandoned. We're called to look for him even in the midst of the darkness. We're called to worship him even through our tears."[15] So writes pastor Pete Wilson in *Plan B*. Even the title of his book reminds us of the fact that God doesn't always behave the way we expect Him to. Nor does He always act when we think it would be the perfect time for Him to respond to prayers and intervene. And, as Job himself would testify, He doesn't always protect us from loss and pain.

In those dark times when the Lord "has taken away," may we choose—as Job himself did—to bless the Lord.

Lord, pain makes it really hard for me to bless You. Of course, I have nowhere else to turn, but sometimes—to be honest—I feel like You are more of an enemy than a friend. Teach me, Lord, to accept from Your hand the hard times as well as the easy times—and to do so graciously. Thank You for the example of Job and the account of Your faithfulness to him in dark times.

ZEPHANIAH 3:17

The LORD your God in your midst,
  The Mighty One, will save;
  He will rejoice over you with gladness,
  He will quiet you with His love,
  He will rejoice over you with singing.

THE LORD YOUR GOD REJOICES IN YOU!

A popular book from several decades ago opened with the blunt statement "Life is difficult"—and who can argue! Yet in the midst of life's difficulties, God blesses us with touches of grace, reasons for joy, and evidence of His love for us. After all, as this verse from Zephaniah reflects, God Himself is a God of joy and gladness and song.

What brings God great joy and genuine pleasure? His people! He delights in those who have pledged their loyalty to Him and recognize His position as almighty God, Author of history, Deliverer, Redeemer, and King. He delights in those people who acknowledge Jesus as their Savior and then choose to serve Him as their Lord. Further delight comes when His people obey Him and when they persevere in their faith during tough and challenging days. God loves when they testify to others of the impact the resurrected Jesus has on their life and when they serve energetically in whatever He calls them to do.

Consider again the wonderful promises of Zephaniah 3:17. First, God is in your midst—in the midst of your schedule, your responsibilities, your home, your workplace, your church, your community, your nation. And this Mighty One will save: He will bring peace, redemption, guidance, and hope to any and every situation you, His child, find yourself in. When you choose to walk in obedience to Him, He will rejoice over you with gladness and song. He will also come alongside to quiet you with His love when circumstances call for that.

The Lord your God is a God of joy. Know that He rejoices in you!

Almighty God, You give me countless reasons to rejoice. You sent Your Son to die for my sin. You gave Your Holy Spirit to be my Teacher, Comforter, and Guide. You created a beautiful world, You bless me with family and friends, and You welcome me into Your eternal family. May I give You reasons to rejoice as well.

PSALM 118:24

❖━━━━━━━━◆━━━━━━━━❖

This is the day the LORD has made;
We will rejoice and be glad in it.

THE LORD ALMIGHTY MADE THIS DAY AND GAVE IT TO YOU.

Ever since Horace penned *carpe diem* ("seize the day") in the first century BC—and probably long before that—philosophers have urged us to make the most of the time we have, and all we have is the present.

"Finish every day and be done with it. . . . This day is all that is good and fair. It is too dear, with its hopes and invitations, to waste a moment on yesterdays."—Ralph Waldo Emerson

"God exists in eternity. The only point where eternity meets time is in the present. The present is the only time there is."—Marianne Williamson

"Don't look back on happiness, or dream of it in the future. You are only sure of today; do not let yourself be cheated out of it."—Henry Ward Beecher

"Life is a great and wondrous mystery, and the only thing we know that we have for sure is what is right here right now. Don't miss it."—Leo Buscaglia

"This is the day the LORD has made; we will rejoice and be glad in it."—The psalmist

These voices from the past and present say basically the same thing, but the psalmist says it best. Why? Because the psalmist gives credit for the gift of today to the Lord, the One who deserves the credit and our thanks.

What will you do to seize today? May what you choose to do and say reflect your gratitude to the Lord who made this day and gave it to you.

Thank You for the gift of this day, Lord God. May I never take for granted that each day of life is indeed a gift—and may I receive that gift not just with gratitude, but with expectancy as well. I want to be looking for Your presence in my life and listening for Your voice, each and every day.

JESUS CALLS YOU TO TRUST HIM—AND

A MUSTARD SEED OF FAITH COUNTS!

MATTHEW 17:20

If you have faith as a
mustard seed, you will
say to this mountain,
"Move from here to
there," and it will move;
and nothing will be
impossible for you.

It's an old hiking trick. It also works for bike riding. And it applies to our faith walk as well.

This is the tip: don't look too far ahead. If the path ahead is rugged and steep, barren and dusty, or stretching out to the horizon to who knows where, the view of the distance can discourage you from going any farther. The prospect of what lies ahead can sap you of energy and enthusiasm; it can totally kill any desire to move ahead.

Life with the Lord is a journey of faith, and sometimes the trail ahead can be less than inviting. The terrain can be hostile and the circumstances less than conducive to forward movement. In fact, the path can look impossible to travel. Perhaps the mountain that stands right in front of you is simply too steep and too rugged, especially for someone with your limited climbing experience. And, yes, by now your feet are very sore. Those hotspots have turned into blisters, you're sure.

When you come to such a point in your faith journey, Jesus calls you to trust Him—and He doesn't require a lot of trust. Jesus calls for faith the size of a mustard seed, and that would be about 1/20 of an inch or, if you prefer metric, 1 to 2 millimeters in diameter. Yes, that is small. Especially next to a mountain.

Sheila Walsh offers this encouragement: "We bring the tiniest seed of faith that God has placed in our spirits, and God honors that faith. If we spend our time looking at the mountain, we will be overwhelmed, so we nurture the seed that God has planted in us."[16]

Lord Jesus, You walked on this earth. You know that we can get tired and our feet can hurt. You know about mountains, both literal and metaphorical. You know how the enemy tries to interfere with my walk of faith. And You know that, despite such challenges, I want to keep walking with You. Thank You for my gift of faith—and thank You that its mustard-seed size won't keep You from handling the mountains in my life.

HEBREWS 4:15–16

We do not have a High Priest
who cannot sympathize with
our weaknesses, but was in
all points tempted as we are, yet
without sin. Let us therefore come
boldly to the throne of grace, that
we may obtain mercy and find
grace to help in time of need.

HAVING WALKED THIS EARTH, JESUS KNOWS
WHAT WE FEEL WHEN WE FACE TEMPTATION.

Native Americans wisely said, "Don't judge any man until you have walked two moons in his moccasins." And there have been many variations on that truth through the generations. An anonymous version is "You never truly know someone until you've walked a mile in his shoes." Elvis Presley tweaked it a bit: "Don't criticize what you don't understand, son. You never walked in that man's shoes." Mahatma Gandhi refined that truth: "Three quarters of the miseries and misunderstandings in the world would finish if people were to put on the shoes of their adversaries and understood their points of view." There is great value in being able to understand another person because you have certain life experiences in common with him or her. That bond does indeed make for a special connection of the heart.

It's possible for us to have that kind of heart connection with Jesus Himself, for He left the throne of heaven and walked this earth for thirty years. The infinite God became finite. He cut teeth and skinned His knees. He learned to walk and talk and work in His father's carpentry shop. More importantly, the writer of Hebrews adds, during His time on this planet, Jesus "was in all points tempted as we are." In other words, He has walked in our moccasins. He truly knows what we feel when we face temptation. He understands, and He will graciously help us stand strong.

That help is not automatic, though. We need to go "boldly to the throne of grace," and, since Jesus knows firsthand the road we're walking, there's no reason for us ever to hesitate.

Lord God, here is yet another reason to praise You for the Incarnation. When Jesus walked on earth—when He walked in my moccasins—He faced temptation. He experienced its power and relentlessness. Yet, Jesus stood strong and taught me that Scripture is the best weapon against the enemy. So may I handle Your Word with skill and confidence whenever temptation strikes.

PSALM 139:16

Your eyes saw my substance,
being yet unformed.
And in Your book they all were written,
The days fashioned for me,
When as yet there were none of them.

OUR SOVEREIGN GOD IS

NEVER SURPRISED BY THE

COURSE OUR LIFE TAKES.

Think about the various hats you wear: wife, mother, Sunday school teacher, Bible study leader, school volunteer, neighbor, cook, cleaner, personal shopper, chauffeur, schedule maker, homework consultant, dog walker—and undoubtedly a couple more equally glamorous responsibilities. Or maybe the following list better reflects your collection of hats: husband, father, youth group rec leader, men's group member, coach, gardener, plumber, home maintenance man, car mechanic, barbecue chef—and you can finish the list.

Or maybe your life is pretty calm right now, and you're enjoying the illusion of control. That illusion, however, can easily be shattered by a traffic accident, an illness, a job layoff, or any other countless, unexpected twists in the road. When we encounter those twists and turns, we do well to remember that we are the ones who find those twists unexpected. Our sovereign God is not surprised; He is never surprised by the course our life takes.

Clearly, David found comfort in this truth. Meditating on God's hand in his life, he reminded himself in this psalm that, even before he was born, "all [his days] were written, the days fashioned for me" by the almighty God. Nothing that happens to us is an accident. No event is beyond God's ability to deliver or redeem. And, by God's grace, no pain or loss will be for naught. So rest in God's sovereignty. Find peace in the fact that your chaotic life is actually under His perfect control.

Sometimes I feel that life is under control; sometimes there's chaos. So I'm thankful for this reminder that You are always in control, Lord God, and that nothing that happens in my life is an unexpected or surprising event to You. Please give me wisdom when it comes to choosing activities. I don't want to contribute to the chaos; I want to be following Your will. But when chaos comes, may I rest in You, knowing that all my days have long been written in Your book.

JOHN 16:33

These things I have spoken to you, that in Me you may have peace. In the world you will have tribulation; but be of good cheer, I have overcome the world.

WHATEVER TRIALS AND TRIBULATIONS YOU FACE, THEY CANNOT DERAIL GOD'S GOOD PLAN FOR YOUR LIFE.

Surely the day can't get any worse! You've undoubtedly had more days like that than you wish. The outfit doesn't work as well as you anticipated, and it's definitely a bad hair day. The toast burns, the coffee spills, the kids don't cooperate. Then the car won't start, or the traffic won't move. Those are frustrations.

Then there are the tribulations. The doctor's diagnosis. The job lost because you took a stand for what was ethical. The unexpected death of a loved one. The estranged friendship. The church split. Jesus promised tribulations, and a sin-stained, fallen world promises frustrations.

When singer Matthew West's flight to an important concert was cancelled, he was more than frustrated. Yet God reminded him of some important truths: "I serve a God who is far greater than a cancelled flight or a missed opportunity. . . . I serve a God who has my best interests at heart at all times. I serve a God who is always at work, orchestrating even the smallest details of my daily life."[17]

Matthew realized that he could do nothing to change the weather and make an airplane fly to where he thought he needed to be. Similarly, you can't unspill the coffee, open up the freeway, or change the doctor's diagnosis. But Matthew chose—as you can—"to rest in knowing that God is not surprised and [that] His plan is still very much intact. So is His plan for your life.

Yes, in this world you will have trouble, but the almighty God has overcome the world!

Lord God, You know the "could it get any worse" circumstances in my life, those situations where I'm feeling overwhelmed. Thank You for this reminder that You are bigger than any circumstances I encounter and that nothing in this world will derail Your good plan for my life. Thank You that You have indeed overcome the world.

GALATIANS 6:4–5

Each person should judge his own actions and not compare himself with others. Then he can be proud for what he himself has done. Each person must be responsible for himself. (NCV)

WE ARE CALLED TO

TEND TO OUR OWN

ACTIONS.

I t may not be a very flattering comparison, but it is a very accurate one: we are fish in water when it comes to recognizing our own sin.

Surrounded by water, a fish is not aware of the weight of the water. Nor is it conscious of the option of life on land, and it does not understand the concept of wetness because water is all it knows. Similarly, being sinners by nature and living in a fallen, sinful world, we are not aware of the weight of sin or even its presence and its wrongness. It's simply the milieu in which we live. Until the Holy Spirit moves in our hearts, we aren't even conscious of the option of what life would be like if we were forgiven of sin and trying to live free of its power. In fact, we don't understand the concept of sin and forgiveness when sin is all we know.

Once the Holy Spirit's freeing, transforming work in us is underway, we can become very aware of sin—yet other people's sin is usually much more obvious to us than our own. Very appropriately, then, here in Galatians 6:4–5, we are called to tend to our own sin. We are warned not to try to be the Holy Spirit for other people. Neither are we quietly to evaluate another's sin and then smugly feel better about ourselves. Instead, let's keep our eyes on Jesus. Gazing on His holiness will help us be more aware of our own sins so that, humbly, we can choose to yield to His transforming work in our lives.

Lord God, I am far too comfortable with my sin and often very blind to it. Forgive me, Lord. Forgive me, too, for feeling superior to people whose sin is so obvious to prideful me. My silent judgments are as wrong as any spoken ones. Continue to do Your convicting, cleansing, and transforming work in me. Continue to keep my focus on Your holy Son.

JOB 23:10

But He knows the way that I take;
When He has tested me,
I shall come forth as gold.

ALLOW GOD'S

POWER TO REFINE

YOU LIKE GOLD.

S ometimes it's a matter of perspective. . . .

Think about a time you were disappointed or hurt. Look back on the relationship that ended, the move that uprooted you, the job loss that impacted the family, the church split that rocked your faith, the premature loss of a loved one to death. By God's grace, the pain and heartache have faded through the years. Has your perspective on that experience changed as well?

You may have come to appreciate what you learned through that hard time. You may see how God used that crisis to move you to where He wanted you to be physically and even spiritually. You might recognize what God was doing in your character, and now you are genuinely thankful for the improvements He made. You might even be able to say that you would never trade in that bittersweet time for anything: bitter because of the pain, that season was nevertheless sweeter than you ever thought possible because of God's almost tangible presence with you each step of the way.

Life's hard times aren't easy. Whichever word you choose— Job chose *tested*, but *pruned*, *refined*, *sanctified*, and *transformed* also work—you can be sure the process will be painful. But by God's redeeming power, the blessings that result from a time of testing can be far greater than you might imagine. In the midst of his devastating losses and the input of his less-than-helpful friends, Job declared, "I shall come forth as gold."

Choose that perspective if you're in the midst of God's testing. Your Redeemer God will not let the pain be for naught.

Grateful that Your power to redeem is unmatched by any pain I encounter on my journey through life, I praise You, almighty God. I praise You that You are always with me, that You use every experience in this fallen world to refine me, to make me more like Christ, that I "shall come forth as gold" for Your glory!

---

1 PETER 3:15

Sanctify the Lord God in your
hearts, and always be ready
to give a defense to everyone
who asks you a reason for
the hope that is in you,
with meekness and fear.

It's not the size of your faith but
the size of your God that matters.

Okay. You may not be Mother Teresa, but you can still have a significant impact on the people around you as you walk with the Lord through life's good times and hard times. Think for a moment about the people God put along your path to bring you to the point of committing your life to Jesus. Think, too, about those individuals He uses even now to encourage you in your faith. Although it's likely that no one you thought of has the far-reaching impact of a Mother Teresa, in God's view every person who came to mind has played an important role in His work of love and redemption.

So what about you? As some wise person once observed, you may be the only Bible some people ever read. No wonder God, through Peter, calls you to "be ready to give a defense to everyone who asks you a reason for the hope that is in you." Are you ready? Writer Angela Elwell Hunt was ready when a friend asked her how she could have been so confident that God would answer her prayer and give her the opportunity to adopt a child. This friend saw that Angela was at peace, trusting that God would send her family the right child at exactly the right time.

Asking how Angela could have been so sure, her friend said, "I don't know if my faith is that big." That is when Angela explained the reason for her hope: "The size of my faith doesn't matter. I'm confident in the size of my God."[18]

Rest in the fact that your God is a very big God—and very able to handle any situations and relationships you care about.

Lord, from time to time, I've asked You to grow my faith. Now I'm thinking that my faith in You can't help but grow as I come to know You better each day. Being aware of Your constant presence with me, Your glory as revealed in Your amazing creation, and Your sovereign hand in world history and my own history will help me appreciate just how big You are. And my faith will grow.

NEHEMIAH 8:10

The joy of the LORD is your strength.

STAY CLOSE TO GOD AND KNOW JOY IN HIM.

Despite having almost twenty-six miles behind them, marathon runners find a boost of energy when the finish line comes into view. Despite the long hours of labor already behind her, the mother finds the ability to push one more time, and her baby is born. Joy in finishing a long race and achieving a goal can give much needed strength in a grueling athletic event. Joy over finally being able to meet the child she already loves is a source of strength in the hospital delivery room. Even more, joy in knowing the Lord is a sure source of strength for His people as they face the challenges, hurts, and disappointments of life.

Jesus offers us the ultimate example of finding strength in the joy of the Lord. Well aware that the cross awaited Him—as well as rejection, mockery, betrayal, denial, and scourging—Jesus was resolved to go to Jerusalem. Luke reported that "He steadfastly set His face to go to Jerusalem" and "His face was set for the journey to Jerusalem" (Luke 9:51, 53). Why was Jesus able to keep moving forward? The author of Hebrews explained that it was because of "the joy that was set before Him" that He "endured the cross" (12:2).

You are undoubtedly bearing a cross of your own. After all, Jesus promised that His people would know trials and tribulations in this world. Yet the joy of the Lord—that "God-given gladness found when we are in communion with God"[19]—truly can sustain you, whatever you're facing. Stay close to your heavenly Father and know joy despite life's circumstances.

When I look to You instead of at my situation, I do indeed find reasons for joy. You, Lord Jesus, are my Savior, Redeemer, and Deliverer. You are my Provider, Protector, and Friend. You are with me always, and nothing can separate me from Your love. You are the sovereign King of kings and, at the same time, my heavenly Father. Yes, You give me many reasons for joy—a joy that will strengthen and sustain me.

INVITE THE

LORD INTO YOUR

SLEEPING HOURS.

PSALM 3:5–6

I lay down and slept;
   I awoke, for the LORD
   sustained me.
I will not be afraid of
   ten thousands of people
Who have set themselves
   against me all around.

A restless night, a bout of insomnia, unsettling dreams—for various reasons, we don't always experience the simple gift of a renewing sleep. Sometimes the cause is physiological, but at other times the reasons are actually a matter of faith.

Are you worried about a situation? Are you stewing over a decision that you need to make? Are you aching over the loss of an important relationship? If sleep doesn't come because of reasons like these, consider inviting the Lord into your sleeping hours, as well as your waking hours.

When you lie in bed awake, stay close to Him. Pray constantly; pray thankfully; pray about everything—and watch for evidence of His presence with you and His work in your life. Also, spend some time laying at His feet any concerns you have, any puzzling situations, and any decisions that are looming large. Confess your worries. Admit your lack of trust.

That simple step of confession may in itself bring peace. If the struggle continues, choose a verse of Scripture to meditate on. You could also ask God to help you recall specific examples of His great faithfulness to you in the past, or you could lay before God's throne of grace any and every concern that is weighing you down and keeping you awake.

When David wrote Psalm 3, he was aware that he was surrounded by enemies who wanted to kill him, but he gave that dangerous situation to God—and he slept. When David awoke, he celebrated the Lord's sustaining power. Follow this example and celebrate the Lord's sustaining power in your life.

Father, You always know the concerns of my heart, even without my saying anything. But when I do pray about those matters, I experience Your peace. So when a day ends, Lord, may I—in faith—let you be on night watch, that in the morning I may celebrate Your sustaining power.

PROCLAIM WITH
YOUR ACTIONS
AND YOUR WORDS,
"I WILL SERVE
THE LORD!"

JOSHUA 24:15

Choose for yourselves this day whom you will serve.... as for me and my house, we will serve the LORD.

Think for a moment about how many choices you have made or will have to make today. Some are pretty minor (what to have for breakfast), whereas other choices may be rather significant (whether to accept that job offer or talk to your elderly parent about assisted-care living). Some decisions are one-time, once-and-for-all: once you decide to be a parent and become one, for instance, you're always a parent. Other decisions need to be made again and again.

The decision to serve the Lord definitely falls into that second category. This choice comes up several times a day as we find ourselves facing the question God asked the people of Israel through Joshua: whom will you serve?

When you could pretend not to see the person with two items heading toward the same cash register . . . When you have learned some shocking but unconfirmed news about an acquaintance and find yourself talking to a friend who would be very interested . . . When your teenager responds to your answer to "What's for dinner?" with "You've gotta be kidding!" . . . When the weak link in the carpool calls yet again, five minutes before you're to meet her at the corner, and says she can't drive this morning . . . Whom will you serve?

With the bigger issues—lying on your tax return, being unfaithful to a spouse, padding expense reports—the choice seems more obvious: Serve God by obeying Him? Or serve yourself? But all those *whens* listed above raise the same issue: Will you serve God by doing the loving, kind, selfless, sacrificial, hard thing? Or will you serve yourself? The choice is yours.

Lord God, I want to choose to serve You. Help me do exactly that—in the simple moments of an ordinary day, as well as in the big issues of life. It truly does make no sense to serve anyone else; yet, too often I choose to serve myself instead of You. Forgive me and, again, help me always choose to serve You.

EPHESIANS 2:8-9

For by grace you have been saved through faith, and that not of yourselves; it is the gift of God, not of works, lest anyone should boast.

HUMBLE YOURSELF,

AND RECEIVE GOD'S

GREAT GIFT.

It doesn't make sense. There's gotta be a catch.

Nope. It's pretty clear in Ephesians: your salvation is a gift. You can't negotiate a peace treaty with the holy God. You can't earn a ticket to heaven. You can't be saved because you perform better than your neighbors on the street—or your neighbors in the pew—because God doesn't grade on a curve. You simply have to believe.

And these are the basics you need to believe in: God is holy. We are sinners. God's Son, Jesus, died on the cross to bridge this gap between God and us. The blood sacrifice of sinless Jesus—His death on the cross—was the punishment He endured for our sin. As a result, now and for eternity, we can live in relationship with God, our heavenly Father and our almighty King.

Those are the basics of the Christian faith. Do you believe? And if you believe, do you realize that even your belief in the gospel truth is a gift? Pastor John MacArthur explains it this way: "Although men are required to believe for salvation, even that faith is part of the gift of God which saves and cannot be exercised by one's own power. God's grace is preeminent in every aspect of salvation."[20]

This gift of the gospel message doesn't make sense to those of us who know there's no such thing as a free lunch, much less a sin-free eternity spent with the Holy God. But there truly is no catch. Simply humble yourself to receive God's gifts of forgiveness, faith, and salvation. Then say thank You by living a life marked by trust, love, and obedience.

Lord God, I would make an excellent Pharisee. I would do a fine job tracking my good deeds and kind words, especially in comparison to what the people around me do and say. But instead You call me to stop striving, to humble myself, and to simply receive Your love. What truly amazing grace!

ISAIAH 41:10

Fear not, for I am with you;
Be not dismayed, for
I am your God.
I will strengthen you,
Yes, I will help you,
I will uphold you with
My righteous right hand.

GOD DECLARES,
"I AM YOUR
GOD, AND I AM
WITH YOU."

I t makes sense: we would not need to be told to "fear not" if there were nothing to fear.

Consider, then, that God Himself—omniscient and eternal—calls us to "fear not." There must be things in this world, in this life, to which fear is a logical and even natural response. What fears have you wrestled with in the past? What fears, if any, are issues for you in the present?

God says, "Fear not," but He doesn't stop with that two-word exhortation. He knows that you can't flip a switch and simply turn off your fear. So He immediately gives the watertight reason to not fear: "for I am with you." What do you know about the great "I AM" that supports His assertion that His presence with you is reason enough not to fear anything?

Maybe, in real time, fear makes that question hard to answer. So God Himself gives you reasons you need not fear: He reminds you that He will provide His people with strength, He will help His people, and He will hold on to His people with His right hand. That right hand represents God's power and His authority over sin as well as His authority over His people. God's hand is a place of complete security.

Despite who God is and His presence with us, dismay and discouragement may come. Why else would God say, "Be not dismayed"? But again God gives a reason to not be dismayed: "I am your God." He is not some distant being; neither is He too busy to attend to you. He declares that He is your God.

So, when you're feeling fearful or dismayed, turn to your God, for He is already with you.

Lord God, burdens are lighter and challenges less overwhelming when I'm not alone. Thank You that, because of You, I am never alone. Because of Your constant presence with me, I do not need to fear or be dismayed. Help me never to be too busy and distracted to call out to You for companionship as well as for guidance or help.

PHILIPPIANS 4:8

Finally, brothers,
whatever is true,
whatever is noble,
whatever is right,
whatever is pure,
whatever is lovely,
whatever is admirable—
if anything is excellent
or praiseworthy—think
about such things. (NIV)

In case you haven't noticed, we live in a very noisy world. Stop reading for a moment and consider all the sounds around you. Do you hear trucks, cars, horns, airplanes, a ringing phone, someone else's conversation, the TV, music from a radio or CD, or all of the above? And then there is the more personal noise we can add to our lives with our iPods, cell phones, and video game headsets.

Now consider what comprises some of that noise: values that aren't in line with God's standards, words that dishonor Him and disrespect other people, ideas that run completely counter to His truth, statements that glorify sin and decadence, arguments for issues that are unbiblical, and the list goes on.

All of this makes obedience to Philippians 4:8 very difficult. It isn't easy to crowd out the noise. And why do inappropriate song lyrics we happen to hear in the grocery store stick with us more easily than the Scripture verse we're trying to memorize?

It makes total sense that God calls on us, His people, to think about whatever is true, noble, right, pure, lovely, admirable, excellent, and praiseworthy. Starting each day by reading His Word will fill our minds with what is worth thinking about. Listening to music that glorifies God will give us a melody to replace the commercial jingle, pop hit, or rap song that is hard to shake. Spending time with fellow believers whose conversation and vocabulary reflect their relationship with God will also keep our thoughts where they should be. Last, but not least, we are wise to ask the Holy Spirit to keep us looking to Jesus, the most excellent and praiseworthy One.

In this noisy world, Lord, help me listen for and hear Your still, small voice. May communing with You keep my mind focused on what is true, noble, right, pure, lovely, admirable, excellent, and praiseworthy. Then use such thoughts, Lord, to direct my words and guide my actions so that I may be Your light in this world darkened by sin.

THE BATTLE
BELONGS TO
THE LORD.

PSALM 28:7-8

The Lord is my strength and my shield;
  My heart trusted in Him, and I am helped;
  Therefore my heart greatly rejoices,
  And with my song I will praise Him.
The Lord is their strength,
  And He is the saving refuge of His anointed.

It's not by chance that battle imagery permeates the Psalms. King David, the author of at least seventy-three of the psalms, was not only a shepherd but also a warrior. He knew the battlefield—its demands, strategies for success, the role that courage and faith play, and which weapons were necessary for victory and survival. No wonder he talks about God and life in military terms in many of his songs.

This battle imagery is even richer for us New Testament believers who know about Jesus' victory over sin, Satan, and death. We have also heard God call us, through the apostle Paul, to "put on the whole armor of God, that you may be able to stand against the wiles of the devil" (Ephesians 6:11). The battle between God and Satan is very real. In Paul's words, "we do not wrestle against flesh and blood, but against principalities, against powers, against the rulers of the darkness of this age, against spiritual hosts of wickedness in the heavenly places" (verse 12).

So David's ancient words acknowledging God as his strength, his shield, and his refuge are as relevant today as they were on the Israelite battlefield centuries ago. God's people in the twenty-first century still need Him to be the source of their strength, their shield of protection from the powers of darkness, and their refuge from the "spiritual hosts of wickedness." Also, God's people would do well to follow David's example of rejoicing in the Lord and praising Him with song. At any point of history, the battle is the Lord's as we yield to Him in faith and with prayer.

My enemies aren't visible. I don't hear the rattling of armor or see sharp spears and hate-filled eyes. But, Lord God, I know the battle rages. Please be my shield as I battle to stand strong in my faith. Thank You that You are my refuge, Lord God, and that I can always go to You to get battle strategies, to sharpen my weapons, and to be refreshed for the next skirmish.

GOD USES PEOPLE OF ALL AGES AND

AT ALL POINTS OF THEIR FAITH

WALK FOR HIS KINGDOM WORK.

1 TIMOTHY 4:12

Let no one despise your youth, but be an example to the believers in word, in conduct, in love, in spirit, in faith, in purity.

We believe our generation is ready to rethink what teens are capable of doing and becoming."[21] So wrote Alex and Brett Harris in *Do Hard Things: A Teenage Rebellion Against Low Expectations* when they were just nineteen. They had been eighteen when they first stood up to "the idea of adolescence as a vacation from responsibility."[22] The theme verse of the Harris brothers' Rebelution movement is 1 Timothy 4:12, a rallying cry to their audience to "be an example to the believers in word, in conduct, in love."

Even if you said good-bye to your teenage years longer ago than you care to think about, both the Harris brothers' examples and the verse from 1 Timothy raise some key issues.

First, what could you be doing to encourage young people as well as new believers to live out their faith, to grow in their knowledge of Jesus, and to be His light in the world? Two thousand years ago the apostle Paul wrote that youth is not to be despised, that God uses people of all ages and at all points of their faith walk for His kingdom work. Ask the Lord to help your attitudes and actions reflect that truth.

Second, whatever your age and wherever you are in your journey of faith, what are you doing to be "an example to the believers in word, in conduct, in love, in spirit, in faith, in purity"? If you're not sure you're doing much of anything, ask Jesus to show you a specific relationship to invest in, a specific sin or character trait to work with Him on changing, or even a specific ministry to get involved in.

Thank You for people like Alex and Brett Harris who call the rest of us to act on Your behalf and to make a difference in this world. And thank You for those young people who are responding to the challenge and being blessed as they are a blessing to those around them. May I, too, be sensitive to where and how you want me to "be an example to the believers in word, in conduct, in love."

GOD, OUR SUN AND
SHIELD, OFFERS US
HIS BLESSINGS.

PSALM 84:11

For the Lord God is a sun and shield;
the Lord bestows favor and honor.
No good thing does he withhold
from those who walk uprightly. (ESV)

I t's no cosmic coincidence: the Earth is the perfect dis-tance from the sun for sustaining life. It's not too close, and it's not too far away. This ideal distance means Earth has water and the right temperatures to support plants and animals. Earth's geography, its 23°27' inclination on its axis, and the speed with which it rotates on that axis—these factors work together to distribute the sun's heat evenly around the planet, another key to sustaining life.[23]

But even without such scientific data available, the psalmist was well aware of some key facts when he wrote "the LORD God is a sun." The psalmist recognized that God is the Source of life, the One who enables us to experience life abundant here on Earth and life eternal with Him. Just as sunlight means health, growth, and light, God's presence means health, growth, and light—physical and spiritual—in the lives of His people.

The psalmist also recognizes God as a shield of protection for those He loves and as the Giver of favor and honor. The favor and honor that God bestows won't be fickle or transitory like the world's. His blessing will, however, vary with His people's obedience: "No good thing does he withhold from those who walk uprightly."

So, to show the Lord your love, walk in obedience to His ways. After all, He is the perfectly distanced sun who gives you life. God in Jesus came close to us when He walked this earth so that we may, through Him, know victory over sin and death, life abundant, and life eternal.

I praise You, Jesus, for bridging the gap between sinful me and the Holy Trinity. By Your incarnation, You came the perfect distance—from heaven to earth—to help me know Your love and Your forgiveness. You modeled humility, service, and sacrificial love. May the life I live for You reflect those same traits. And may God, like the sun, prompt spiritual health and growth in me, that I might give Him glory.

HEBREWS 12:1-2

Since we are surrounded by
so great a cloud of witnesses,
let us lay aside every weight,
and the sin which so easily
ensnares us, and let us run
with endurance the race
that is set before us, looking
unto Jesus, the author and
finisher of our faith.

Fix your eyes on
Jesus; then run the
race before you.

As the author of Hebrews points out, several things can keep us from running a good race in this life. Believers in his first-century audience were, for instance, burdened by the impossible-for-everyone-except-Jesus-to-satisfy law of God. By His grace, we New Testament believers find ourselves free of that, but instead we may be lugging around heavy burdens of self-made laws, regret, hurt, and worry. We can also be tripped up by sin, and we can choose to believe the lie that we can't run another step. Consider the better option: looking to Jesus!

Jenna Lucado realized the futility of trying to find security in people's approval—it only made her feel more insecure and dissatisfied with herself—so she changed her focus. In *Redefining Beautiful*, she wrote this: "I really started to feel secure when I started to focus on God. People will always make mistakes, have biased opinions, or just not be there all of the time. But God is the one who will never leave, the home that will never be destroyed, and the family that won't be broken."

Sharing a valuable lesson she learned the hard way, Jenna calls us to fix our eyes on Jesus. "Taking your eyes off of yourself and turning them onto the One who loves you"[24] is the key to knowing security, joy, and hope in this life. Fixing our eyes on Jesus can also help us keep our priorities straight and simplify our day because we know where we're going, why we're going, and whom we're going with. Such simplicity and security are blessings indeed.

Responsibilities, fun, work, family members, neighbors, friends, physical ailments, worries, my sinful choices, and plain old noise can distract me, Lord, and keep me from focusing on Jesus. He alone is the source of unfailing love and genuine security. He alone gives sure guidance and unshakable joy. I know that, but I don't always live it. Please forgive me when I look elsewhere for purpose and significance.

REVELATION 21:4

God will wipe away every tear from their eyes; there shall be no more death, nor sorrow, nor crying. There shall be no more pain, for the former things have passed away.

GOD DRAWS NEAR TO THE HUMBLED, HURTING HEART.

Jesus didn't try to sugarcoat the truth. He told His followers—He has told us—that we will encounter trials and tribulations during our four score years on this planet. Loss and betrayal will be a part of our lives as they were for Jesus Himself. We will be lonely and misunderstood as He was. We may be falsely accused and treated unfairly, and Jesus knows about that firsthand as well. We will be frustrated when people don't understand our commitment to the Lord (Jesus' own disciples were baffled and slow to understand what He was all about), and we may often struggle to accept God's will (remember Jesus in Gethsemane). It's no surprise, then, that the path we walk on this earth is watered with our tears.

God knows those tears. He is with us always, whatever storms come our way and whatever darkness blinds us to His presence. He is the God of all compassion and comfort. He knows that locusts descend, and He restores the blessings lost during those years of blight. He knows that the fires of life can ravage His people, and He brings beauty out of ashes. God knows when we cry, and He draws near to the humbled, hurting heart.

More wonderful than the truth that God knows our tears and collects them in a bottle (Psalm 56:8) is the fact that one day He "will wipe away every tear." What a picture of His tender love! And one day there will be no more tears, "no more death, nor sorrow, nor crying . . . no more pain." What a picture of a redeemed world!

Come quickly, Lord!

I've heard it said that pain is never wasted in Your economy, and Your Word supports that truth. You do redeem the years of the locust (Joel 2:25). You do bring beauty out of ashes (Isaiah 61:3). You come alongside Your people with comfort and compassion (2 Corinthians 1:3; James 5:11). Even as I praise You, God, I look forward to the day of Your total victory over sin, death, sorrow, crying, and pain.

PROVERBS 3:5–6

Trust in the LORD with all your heart,
  And lean not on your own understanding;
In all your ways acknowledge Him,
  And He shall direct your paths.

S adly, we can listen to words but not actually hear them, just as we can look at people but not really see them. Similarly, we can become blind to beauty we see all the time and numb to truths we hear all the time. We can become lukewarm about one-time passions and self-reliant rather than God dependent when life is going well. In light of these facts about human nature, read again Proverbs 3:5–6. Try to hear the words and come alive to the truth.

Perhaps rereading the familiar wording is not as effective as hearing the ideas stated in a slightly different way. That is what Sarah Young offers in *Jesus Calling*: "Strive to trust Me in more and more areas of your life. Anything that tends to make you anxious is a growth opportunity. . . . If you believe that I am sovereign over every aspect of your life, it is possible to trust Me in all situations. . . . Trust is like a staff you can lean on, as you journey uphill with Me. If you are trusting in Me consistently, the staff will bear as much of your weight as needed."[25]

EMBRACE OPPORTUNITIES TO LEARN TO TRUST THE LORD WITH ALL YOUR HEART.

Confess what, if anything, you are feeling anxious about right now. In what areas of your life are you struggling to trust Jesus? In what current situation do you need to lean more heavily on the staff of trust? Ask the Lord to reignite your passion for Him, to help you recognize and release any self-reliant attitudes and habits, and to embrace the growth opportunities that life brings your way.

Thank You, Holy Spirit, for helping me hear afresh familiar truths. And thank You that You can help grow my faith and transform me into a more trusting follower of Jesus. I do want to lean more heavily on the staff; I do want to release my self-reliant attitudes and habits and instead fully depend on God for strength, direction, and joy.

2 TIMOTHY 1:7

God has not given us a spirit of fear, but of power and of love and of a sound mind.

GOD'S PERFECT LOVE FOR US CASTS OUT FEAR.

The twenty-first century is characterized in the West by a spirit of pseudo tolerance (let's tolerate every faith except Christianity) and hypersensitivity about offending people (who aren't Christians). Believers in other parts of the world actually face imprisonment, torture, and death for their faith in Jesus. So, just as in the first century of the church, twenty-first-century believers need to be encouraged to proclaim and defend the gospel, making Paul's reminder to Timothy as relevant as ever.

The apostle's charge begins with "God has not given us a spirit of fear." Such fear reflects a lack of faith in God's sovereignty, protection, and love, and God's perfect love for us casts out that fear (1 John 4:18). It is a tool the enemy uses—and uses skillfully—to discourage God's people from taking a bold, confident stand in Him and for Him. So when fear rises, rebuke the enemy in the powerful name of Jesus and act for the Lord and His truth despite the fear.

Paul then reminded Timothy that, rather than giving His people the spirit of fear, God has blessed us with power, love, and a sound mind. The Spirit will give us the strength to speak boldly and the energy to speak at every opportunity that presents itself. When God calls us to ministry of any and every kind, He empowers us to do that ministry. The Spirit will also enable us to love with God's love those people with whom we are sharing the gospel truth. Finally, the Spirit provides us with the ability to think clearly and to know when it is appropriate to minister or witness with our words and when it is not.

You, Lord, are stronger than he who is in the world. May we who love You—may I—trust in the presence and power of Your Spirit and boldly share the truth about salvation in Jesus and in Him alone. I want to stand strong in Your power and love and glorify You as I point people to Your Son, my Savior.

GLORY IN THE
FACT THAT YOU
KNOW THE LORD!

JEREMIAH 9:23–24

"Let not the wise man glory in his wisdom,
  Let not the mighty man glory in his might,
  Nor let the rich man glory in his riches;
But let him who glories glory in this,
  That he understands and knows Me,
  That I am the LORD, exercising lovingkindness,
    judgment, and righteousness in the earth.
For in these I delight," says the LORD.

Wisdom, power, and wealth—God warns us against pridefully finding glory in these, yet we aren't listening. Graduate and honorary degrees reflect a certain amount of learning and accomplishment but not necessarily wisdom. Strength can be indicated by athletic records, workout hours at the gym, pounds bench-pressed, and miles run, but strength is fleeting. Both a sudden injury and gradual aging can take their toll. Riches can be measured by possessions and bank accounts, but fire and international economics can steal these away. Still, we gravitate toward the honor that comes when we are regarded as wise, mighty, or rich.

Consider, however, that God calls us to glory in the fact that we know and understand Him. That is a rather mind-boggling reality—you have been invited to know and to be in relationship with the Creator, Sustainer, and sovereign Ruler of the universe. Knowing Him means seeing Him when others don't, seeing when He is indeed "exercising lovingkindness, judgment, and righteousness in the earth." You see His lovingkindness in the way He faithfully answers your prayers and provides for all your needs. You find hope and peace in the truth that He will one day exercise judgment against the immoral and ungodly. You see His righteousness in His commands, and you look forward to the ultimate victory when Jesus returns to reign in righteousness.

What a privilege to know all facets of the Lord! May your time spent reading God's Word, worshiping the Lord, and praying to Him—each of which is truly a privilege—bring you great joy day in and day out.

You know, Father, how powerful the attraction of the world's so-called wisdom, power, and wealth can be. I know I am vulnerable and easily pulled away from You. I am easily distracted from godly wisdom, the power of love and sacrifice, and wealth that lasts for eternity. Thank You for Scripture that calls me back to You.

ROMANS 8:28–29

We know that in all things God works for the good of those who love him, who have been called according to his purpose. For those God foreknew he also predestined to be conformed to the likeness of his Son, that he might be the firstborn among many brothers. (NIV)

"GOD WORKS FOR THE GOOD OF THOSE WHO LOVE HIM."

Happily ever after has a wonderful ring to it, and many people do their best to try to secure that happy ending. They have their rabbit foot, their lucky hat, or their not-to-be-varied pregame routine. Some of us Christians don't worry about having a rabbit's foot, but we do grab onto Romans 8:28 as something of a good luck charm. After all, it says, "We know that in all things God works for the good of those who love him." What a glorious guarantee of a happily-ever-after life for those who call Jesus "Lord"!

But is this verse truly a happily-ever-after promise? Look again at the end of Romans 8:28 and the verse it introduces: "who have been called according to his purpose. For those God foreknew he also predestined to be conformed to the likeness of his Son." God works for the good of those who love Him (criterion #1) and whom He has called according to His purpose for them (criterion #2). Verse 29 explains that purpose: God wants His people to become more like Jesus.

Jesus is sinless, holy, and pure. Jesus is patient and kind; He is not envious, boastful, rude, self-centered, irritable, or evil thinking. Jesus hates iniquity. He loves truth. No matter what came His way on this earth, He bore all things, believed all things, hoped all things, and endured all things (see 1 Corinthians 13:4–7). Where do you see yourself in that mirror of Scripture?

God uses every event, relationship, challenge, and hurt that we experience to make us more like Jesus. No one can improve on that happily ever after.

Lord God, I am humbled by this reminder of Your great purpose for me: You want me to be more like Jesus. You care more about my Christlikeness than my happiness. May I, like Jesus Himself, submit to Your will and cooperate with Your transforming work so that I can glorify You in this life.

GOD'S GRACE IS

FAR GREATER THAN

ALL YOUR SIN.

PSALM 51:1–2

Have mercy upon me, O God,
 According to Your lovingkindness;
 According to the multitude of
  Your tender mercies,
 Blot out my transgressions.
Wash me thoroughly from my iniquity,
 And cleanse me from my sin.

Isn't it interesting how much more easily we see other people's sin than our own! Then, for whatever reasons (sin?, pride? something else equally ungodly?), we also do a fine job of rank ordering the sin we see in other people: "Her sin of x is far worse than his sin of y and my sin of z!" But every sin ever committed—your sins included—sent Jesus to the cross.

The sins of King David, a man after God's own heart and the author of Psalm 51, also sent Jesus to the cross. And among those sins were adultery, deception, framing a loyal military leader, murder, cover-up, and pride. As pastor Andy Stanley has pointed out, "If grace had limits, David's behavior would have exposed them."

But David isn't the only one through the centuries who has needed God's grace in a big way.

Andy put it this way: "We've all put God's grace to the test. We have broken his law. We've been irresponsible with his blessing. We've confessed a sin only to turn right around and repeat it. It's those occasions when I begin to wonder, *How many times? How many times can I expect God to forgive me for the same sin? . . . Where does grace end and retribution begin?* If David's story is any indication, grace has no end. . . . Regardless of what you've done, regardless of how far you've strayed, regardless of how long it's been since you addressed God directly, regardless of what you've been told, regardless of how you feel, grace awaits you. Grace that is far greater than all your sin!"[26]

And that is very good news!

"Grace that is far greater than all your sin!" That truth is balm for the soul, Lord God. I struggle like the apostle Paul did: I do what I don't want to do, and I don't do what I want to do. I get frustrated with myself, and I'm sure You get frustrated with me too. So, since I'm still very much in process, it is good to know that You will never run out of grace for me.

---

2 CORINTHIANS 5:17

If anyone is in Christ, he is a new creation; old things have passed away; behold, all things have become new.

WHAT A PRIVILEGE TO BE "IN CHRIST" AND TRANSFORMED TO BE MORE LIKE JESUS!

The truth of 2 Corinthians 5:17 is made meaningful to Sunday school students with the illustration of a butterfly. After all, this one-time caterpillar has become a new creation. The transformation was not immediate; the process took time. And if the butterfly could speak, it might think back on the process as being somewhat mysterious. What was going on? Why did it have to go through the dark season of isolation when nothing of value seemed to be happening? But in the end, the new creation was glorious. No longer confined to crawling on the ground, the butterfly knew the freedom of flight.

The truth of 2 Corinthians 5:17 is made meaningful to adults not only through the butterfly analogy but also through the teaching of such Bible scholars as John MacArthur. He calls the two words *in Christ* the "most profound statement of the inexhaustible significance of the believer's redemption." And that redemption—that newness *in Christ*—changes us just as that caterpillar was changed: "After a person is regenerate, old value systems, priorities, beliefs, loves, and plans are gone. Evil and sin are still present, but the believer sees them in a new perspective, and they no longer control him."[27]

Still needing to stand strong against sin but freed from its control, redeemed believers are new creations. Redeemed believers have adopted their Lord's values and priorities. They are open to His ongoing transformational work in their lives so that, like that butterfly, they can enjoy the freedom that comes with the forgiveness, love, and grace God continuously pours out on His people.

Lord God, thank You for Your plan of redemption, achieved through Jesus' sacrificial death on the cross for my sin. And thank You for the transforming work You have begun and continue to do in my life. Grow in me a greater sensitivity to Your guiding Spirit, that I may live a life that reflects Your goodness and love.

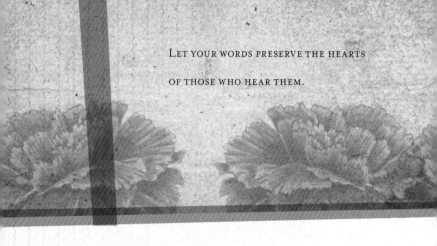

LET YOUR WORDS PRESERVE THE HEARTS

OF THOSE WHO HEAR THEM.

COLOSSIANS 4:6

Let your speech always be
with grace, as though seasoned
with salt, so that you will
know how you should respond
to each person. (NASB)

Words are powerful. God spoke the universe into existence. Satan spoke words of deceit to Eve that led to the entrance of sin into the world. Jesus spoke life-changing words of forgiveness and healing. Paul wrote words of encouragement and instruction. Ananias and Sapphira spoke untrue words that cost them their lives. Words are powerful for good and for bad; they can build people up or tear them down.

Think about words you remember from your childhood, a favorite professor, a longtime friend, or Scripture. Perhaps the negatives have stuck with you more than the positives, and that is a sobering thought. Just as another person's less-than-gracious words have stuck with you, some of yours may have stuck with other people. Words we have spoken have either built people up or torn them down. Those are basically the only two options.

In Colossians 4:6, God calls us to the positive option: He instructs us to season our speech with grace just as we season our food with salt. Used in moderation, salt enhances the taste of food. Salt has also been used as a preservative through the centuries. Adding grace to our speech should have the same effect that salt has on food. Specifically, the grace of our words can and should enhance our message and preserve rather than destroy the hearts of those to whom we speak.

Consider the impact your words generally have on the people you talk to. May the indwelling Holy Spirit bless us with self-control and the ability to think before we speak so that our speech will "always be with grace."

Lord God, this truth is simple enough to understand, but so very hard to live out. Too often I speak before I think. Too often I am guilty of having that untamable tongue that James taught about (3:5–12). I struggle to control my tongue, and at times I even struggle to want to speak kindly and constructively. Forgive me, Lord, transform me, and teach me to speak only words that You want me to speak.

THE FATHER
IS PLEASED BY
GODLY HEARTS
AND GODLY
ATTITUDES.

PSALM 19:14

Let the words of my mouth
and the meditation of my heart
Be acceptable in Your sight,
O LORD, my strength and my Redeemer.

GIGO. Garbage in; garbage out. This basic principle in computer programming asserts that the quality of the output is directly related to and dependent on the quality of the input. If the program is flawed, the information it produces will be flawed. If the data entered into a perfectly fine program is faulty, then the information the program produces will be faulty. Makes perfect sense, doesn't it?

A word of caution. Sometimes a little bit of garbage can have a huge impact on the outcome. Do you remember when one "little goof" cost NASA a $125-million Mars probe? The mistake was simple enough: some engineers were using inches and feet; others were using metric. Oops! GIGO!

Can you think of where else this principle might apply? Yep, a look in the mirror shows each of us another place where the GIGO principle consistently functions. When we put garbage into our hearts and minds, we shouldn't be surprised when garbage comes out. But let's focus on the positive corollary here: if what we put into our heart and mind is godly and pure, what comes out of us—our words, actions, attitudes, and thoughts—will be much more pleasing to God.

Garbage in . . . *I don't see R-rated movies very often. . . . I know what's right and wrong. That television show isn't going to influence me. . . . Yeah, the lyrics are awful, but the song is so catchy. . . .* Garbage out! So pray with David: "Let the words of my mouth and the meditation of my heart be acceptable in Your sight!"

Lord God, I do want my thoughts, words, attitudes, and actions to glorify You. Please help me choose to fill my mind and heart with good, not garbage, so that good comes out more often than garbage does. Lead me not into temptation as I choose activities, music, movies, books, magazines, and friends. Help me, Spirit, to exercise self-control and be sensitive to Your guidance. I do want to glorify You, Father God!

OUR HEAVENLY

FATHER KNOWS

EXACTLY

WHAT WE, HIS

CHILDREN, NEED.

PHILIPPIANS 4:19

This same God who
takes care of me will
supply all your needs
from his glorious riches,
which have been given to
us in Christ Jesus. (NLT)

Needs versus wants. In our culture and age of entitlement, the line between the two has been blurred. Yet, it's an important distinction for all of us when it comes to both praying to our heavenly Father and understanding the promise of Philippians 4:19.

Perhaps the verse is a statement of the obvious, but Jesus felt it worthwhile to remind us that the Lord knows exactly what we, His children, need. Aware of our tendency to worry about what we will eat and what we will wear, Jesus declared, "Your heavenly Father knows that you need all these things" (Matthew 6:32). That being said, we can trust Him to meet those needs. The food may not be gourmet; the clothes may not be designer. But any expectations of filet mignon and Gucci labels reflect our desires rather than our needs.

And the apostle Paul—an itinerant preacher for a movement unpopular among both the Jewish leaders of his day and the politically powerful Romans—knew what it was like to be in need. So, when the faithful members of the church at Philippi sent Paul a sacrificial gift in support of his ministry, he thanked them as well as the Lord. Then Paul went on to encourage those brothers and sisters with the truth of Philippians 4:19.

Gracious and generous, our heavenly Father continues to provide for His children out of His infinite resources. He faithfully meets our needs, and He often does so in ways far greater than we would have imagined.

Father God, You sent Your Son to die on the cross for my sins. You enabled me to recognize the truth of the gospel. You welcomed me into relationship with You. And despite all You have done for me, I still find it easier to doubt than to trust. Forgive me, Lord, and thank You for reminding me that You will indeed meet all my needs in this life and for eternity.

ISAIAH 40:12-13

Who has measured the waters in
the hollow of His hand,
Measured heaven with a span
And calculated the dust of the
earth in a measure?
Weighed the mountains in scales
And the hills in a balance?
Who has directed the Spirit of the Lord,
Or as His counselor has taught Him?

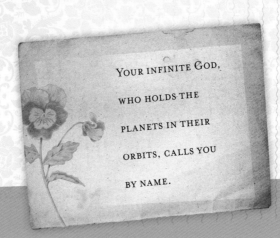

YOUR INFINITE GOD,
WHO HOLDS THE
PLANETS IN THEIR
ORBITS, CALLS YOU
BY NAME.

The heavens do declare the glory of God (Psalm 19:1)! They speak of His majesty, His power, His design, and even His love. Such was the experience of author Donald Miller when he visited the Grand Canyon. Lying on the ground that clear night and staring into the heavens, he marveled at the starry host sparkling in the dark sky above him: "There is something beautiful about a billion stars held steady by a God who knows what He is doing."

Then the beauty of God's presence became very personal: "The knowledge of God seeped out of my brain and into my heart. I imagined Him looking down on this earth, half angry because His beloved mankind had cheated on Him, had committed adultery, and yet hopelessly in love with her, drunk with love for her."[28]

The order of the heavens, the complexity of a DNA molecule, the miracle of birth, the beauty of color and music and light—everywhere we turn we see our Creator God's fingerprints in this world. Those fingerprints speak not only of His existence but also of His ongoing involvement in His creation and, more importantly, of His love not just for His mankind in general but His love for you in particular.

Yes, our infinite God holds the planets in their orbits, but He also calls you by name and numbers the hair on your head (Isaiah 43:1; Matthew 10:30). What amazing love! Take some time today to get outdoors, be alone with your Father, and listen for what He has to say just to you.

Father God, You are vast and wonderful beyond measure! Thank You for this moment today to pause and consider Your amazing creation. Whenever I make time to worship You in the beautiful outdoors, whenever I pause to marvel at Your handiwork and Your sustaining power that is so evident in the created world, help me also to listen for Your voice and Your words of direction, peace, and love.

MATTHEW 6:33

Seek first the kingdom of God and His righteousness, and all these things shall be added to you.

IS YOUR NUMBER ONE

PRIORITY ALLOWING

GOD TO REIGN IN

YOUR LIFE?

S eek first the kingdom of God." Simple to understand, but not always easy to live out, right?

This description fits many of Jesus' commands. *Love God with all that you are. Love your neighbor as yourself. Treat others the way you want to be treated. Pray always; pray persistently. Give thanks in everything.* In most instances, we understand exactly what Jesus means, but obeying Him is a very different matter.

Part of Jesus' Sermon on the Mount, the instruction to seek God's kingdom comes near the end of a teaching that touched on wealth, worries, and trust. Knowing human nature, Jesus cautioned His audience—then and now—against focusing on worldly acquisitions, and He warned that no one can serve God and money at the same time. Jesus also knew how readily we worry about basic life necessities, so He reminded His listeners that God will take care of them just as He takes care of the birds of the air. As the culminating point of His argument, Jesus declared that God knows His people's needs and will provide for those needs. On the heels of that truth came the command to "seek first the kingdom of God and His righteousness" with the promise that "all these things shall be added to you."

So are things eternal your main focus as you plan your schedule? Is your number one priority allowing God to reign in your life? Or are you more concerned about "all these things"? Of course these "things"—food, clothes, paying bills—need to be attended to. But if you need to choose between the two, will you take the step of faith and let God's kingdom pull rank?

Lord, the longer I walk with You, the more I realize how much You care about the condition of my heart. And I'm very aware that my heart is not always right, even when my actions are. So, please cleanse, purify, and transform my heart. I want to be Your person inside and out, every day of the week, every minute of the day.

PSALM 127:1

Unless the LORD builds the house,
They labor in vain who build it;
Unless the LORD guards the city,
The watchman stays awake in vain.

WE ARE INVITED

INTO A MARVELOUS

PARTNERSHIP WITH GOD.

The principle worked in college, especially during final exam time: "Study like you don't pray—and pray like you don't study."

That rule of thumb for students reflects a principle that King Solomon set forth in Psalm 127 several millennia ago. Simply put, we need to give our best effort to the task God has given us to do. At the same time, we need to be praying faithfully and fervently about that task, asking God for His guidance, His strength, and His blessing. Anything we do—especially any kingdom work we undertake—in our own power, for our own glory, is destined to either fail or at least fall far short of what the result would have been with the Almighty's blessing.

Also reflected in King Solomon's wisdom is the marvelous partnership God invites us into. We are to labor to the best of our abilities and fulfill the responsibilities God assigns us. But we are to put forth our efforts for God and His glory. We are to trust that He will show us what to do, enable us to do it, and bless our work. But if we're building a house that God hasn't called us to build, we "labor in vain." If we are going in a direction opposite of what God would choose for us, we travel in vain.

What house, if any, are you building right now that may not be God's will for you? What task, if any, are you working hard at but without the Lord's involvement or a sense of His presence with you? Ask those questions of God. Listen for His answer. Then trust Him as you obey Him.

Almighty Lord, it truly is amazing that You, Creator and Omnipotent God, allow us to partner with You in Your kingdom work. You invite us and empower us—and warn us that if we set out in our own direction and under our own power, we serve You in vain. Show me where, if at all, I'm working independently of You and outside of Your will. And please show me specifically where You would have me enjoy the privilege of serving You.

MARK 8:34–36

Whoever desires to come after Me, let him deny himself, and take up his cross, and follow Me. For whoever desires to save his life will lose it, but whoever loses his life for My sake and the gospel's will save it. For what will it profit a man if he gains the whole world, and loses his own soul?

IF WE DENY OURSELVES, WE CAN LIVE FOR CHRIST.

We can and do respond to invitations in various ways. Maybe you don't really want to attend a party, but you definitely want to be invited! Or you desperately want to attend, but the invitation doesn't come. For another event, an unwanted invitation comes, and you know that attending is the right thing to do.

Think about your initial response to Jesus' invitation in Mark 8:34–36: take up your cross and follow Me. Especially in Jesus' day, but even twenty-one centuries later, the cross meant agony and death. It was the Romans' excruciatingly painful way of eliminating criminals and enemies of the state. The cross was an instrument of torture and shame. These facts make taking up our own cross a less than appealing proposition, but accepting the invitation is inherent in our decision to follow Jesus.

We cannot live for ourselves, according to our own desires and dreams, and follow Jesus at the same time. By His grace, though, Jesus' plans for us may match our desires and dreams, but His plans may also include the painful exercise of dying to our own ideas about the course of our lives.

Read Sheila Walsh's perspective on what it means to take up your cross: "It means that every time my will crossed God's will, I dragged my will back in line with His. It means doing the things that I know are good and true, whether I feel like it or not. It means setting my face and heart toward heaven just as Jesus did. . . . We study how Jesus lived, how He loved, and follow His example. When we find ourselves in a difficult place, we do what He did: we turn to our Father."[29]

Calling You "Lord" implies my willingness to no longer be in charge of my own life. When I'm struggling with that, help me keep my eyes on You, knowing that You will bless my obedient yielding to Your will. You will bless the journey, protect my soul, and one day welcome me into Your heavenly kingdom.

Knowing God's Word and obeying it keeps us on God's narrow path.

JOSHUA 1:8

This book of the law shall not depart from your mouth, but you shall meditate on it day and night, so that you may be careful to do according to all that is written in it; for then you will make your way prosperous, and then you will have success. (NASB)

No one likes to be lost. Consider how popular GPS (global positioning system) devices have become. People have the gadgets in their cars and the app on their cell phones. A GPS prevents wrong turns, backtracking, aimless wandering, and even spousal arguments and frustration. These handy devices determine the best route and provide clear directions, allowing drivers and passengers to enjoy the ride.

God's Word serves as something of a GPS device for His people. Knowing His Word and obeying it can keep us on the path God wants us to walk. We need only to hide its truth in our heart so that we can detect falsehood and spin. The world offers its temptations and distractions, and the enemy is subtle and persuasive in his deceitful schemes. In addition, many people today and the culture in general are hostile to Christianity and growing more so. Staying on God's narrow path is becoming more and more difficult, but that is nothing new.

Consider the four-thousand-year-old message Joshua spoke to God's people: know Scripture, meditate on the Lord's truth, be careful to obey His commands, and know His blessing. Those words are just as relevant and life-giving today. And now, on this side of the cross, believers have not only the written Word to direct them but also the example of Christ as well as the indwelling Holy Spirit to provide guidance and strength for the journey of life. God has given His people all they need to walk in His way, for all time.

~~~~~~~~

Thank You for all You have given me to guide me in life. Thank You for the specific guidance I find in Your written Word, for the example of Jesus Himself whose every moment of life honored and glorified You, and for Your Holy Spirit who convicts, guides, and empowers. Lord, please enable me to make choices that will keep me walking on the path of life.

~~~~~~~~

PHILIPPIANS 3:12–14

Not that I have already attained, or
am already perfected; but I press on,
that I may lay hold of that for which
Christ Jesus has also laid hold of
me. Brethren, I do not count myself
to have apprehended; but one thing I
do, forgetting those things which
are behind and reaching forward to
those things which are ahead, I press
toward the goal for the prize of the
upward call of God in Christ Jesus.

ACCEPT GOD'S FORGIVENESS, AND

PRESS ON TOWARD THE GOAL.

I'm not sure where I'm going, but I'm making good time." That comment may elicit a smile, but it's not a statement anyone would want on a tombstone.

Do you know where you're going on this journey of life? The apostle Paul did. His previous destination had been Damascus, where he planned to purge the city of those Jesus followers who threatened the purity of the Jewish faith. But after meeting the risen Lord on the road to the city, the apostle had a new and clearly defined mission.

He was determined to share the good news that the long-awaited Jewish Messiah had in fact arrived. Like many other Jews, Paul had failed to recognize Him, but now Paul knew better. God had indeed sent His only Son as a sacrifice for the sin of every one of us—past, present, and future. That was news worth sharing, and Paul tackled the assignment wholeheartedly.

We could let ourselves be bogged down by our past sin, but we can do nothing to change what has already been done. We need to move on as Paul did, accepting God's forgiveness and serving Christ with all that we are. A laser-sharp focus on Jesus can keep current responsibilities in perspective.

The apostle Paul had an overriding priority that guided his steps, and that paramount concern was to serve Jesus the Christ. By God's grace, may the same be said of us. May the goal of serving Jesus in whatever capacity He calls us be a plumb line for our lives. After all, we truly do have a Savior worth serving with all our heart, soul, mind, and strength.

Lord God, thank You for calling me to know Jesus as my Savior and Lord. Thank You for the privilege of serving Him as I journey through life. May I keep that high calling my main focus despite the responsibilities and concerns of the present and anything from the past that may slow me down. May I—like Paul—"press toward the goal for the prize of the upward call of God in Christ Jesus."

ROMANS 8:26

The Spirit also helps in our weaknesses. For we do not know what we should pray for as we ought, but the Spirit Himself makes intercession for us with groanings which cannot be uttered.

THE HOLY SPIRIT HELPS

WHEN WE DON'T HAVE

WORDS OF OUR OWN.

I t's a lesson we don't learn early on or easily.

We stay away from people who are hurting or grieving because we don't know what to say to them. Eventually some of us learn—maybe from times when we ourselves are suffering—that a person's presence is more significant than words. Our being with someone who is going through hard times speaks eloquently of love and concern; the hurting person doesn't need clichés or possible explanations or, at times, even Scripture verses.

When we are hurting, we know that no one's words can make the situation better, the heart less heavy, or the tears stop flowing. In fact, we don't always have words of our own to cry out to the Lord. The hurt is just too deep.

That was the case of pastor Pete Wilson during the days and weeks after his wife's miscarriage. He wrote, "I remember thinking, *Spirit, I need you to pray for me. While I grieve, you pray. While I long for things to be different, you pray. While I wait for hope, you pray . . . because I just can't.*"

It was some time before Pete could and did pray, but God was at work. "Looking back, I can see that it was in that very act of saying 'I can't' that I began to heal. I was . . . finally relinquishing control. . . . Giving up control is difficult and even painful, but it makes room for God to work, healing us from past pain and helping us move forward, hopefully, into a fresh future."[30]

The Spirit prays for us even as He comforts us and as God does His work of healing and sowing seeds of hope.

———

Holy Spirit, You have comforted me on many occasions. You have also blessed me with peace when circumstances foster inner chaos. As wonderful as those gifts are, probably the most significant aspect of Your ministry is the fact that You pray for me. Whether pain overwhelms me, a situation perplexes me, or I need to make a tough decision, You know how to pray—and You do pray. Thank You.

———

1 PETER 5:6–7

Humble yourselves under the mighty hand of God, that He may exalt you in due time, casting all your care upon Him, for He cares for you.

<small>Godly humility brings freedom, hope, and a greater awareness of the Almighty's very real love.</small>

The word *humble* is related to the word *humus*, that partially decomposed stuff we put in our gardens to help the plants grow. Both words are rooted in the Latin *humilis*, meaning "low." And that information hardly makes God's call to humility appealing, does it?

The word *humility* can bring to mind such negative associations as the unhealthy choice to be a doormat for others or the "I don't care, whatever you want is fine with me" person. But none of that is biblical, godly, or Christlike humility. As Paul wrote in Philippians 2:8, Jesus "humbled Himself and became obedient to the point of death, even the death of the cross." Jesus' choice of humility meant submitting to God's authority and the eternal plan that involved the Incarnation with its aspects of crucifixion, death, and total separation from God.

Jesus' willingness to submit to God's plan—"Thy will be done"—is an example to us. As Paula Rinehart says, "To humble yourself is to surrender to the authority of God in your life. 'Okay, Lord, I give in. I take my place as your well-loved child. You know what is best for me.' There is something enormously freeing about a humility that recognizes and surrenders to God. . . . As I rest under the mighty hand of God, I let Him carry the weight of my life. My hope is planted in the reality that He cares for me—pure and simple."[31]

Simple to understand, but not easy to live out. Yet, God Himself will enable you to humble yourself under His authority and then to experience the freedom that comes with surrendering to Him.

Lord God, it's interesting to think about the relationship between the words humility *and* humus. *Perhaps just as humus helps plants grow, my humility can help my faith in You grow. Show me, I ask, the way of humility and enable me to walk that path— by Your grace and according to Your kingdom plan.*

JOHN 10:10

I have come that they may have life, and that they may have it more abundantly.

LIFE ABUNDANT

COMES WHEN WE

WALK IN GOD'S WAYS.

These days, very few of us have spent much time with sheep, and even fewer of us are shepherds; however, we easily understand Jesus' point in a passage about sheep, a thief, and a shepherd, the passage that John 10:10 comes from.

Guarding the sheep pen, especially at night, is essential, because those who visit the pen under cover of darkness are up to no good. As Jesus put it, "the thief does not come except to steal, and to kill, and to destroy" (John 10:10). Those are the goals not just of a sheep robber in Jesus' day, but also of Satan today. This enemy of almighty God carefully schemes and slyly works to steal away from God the people He loves, people He longs to adopt into His eternal family. Satan tries to convince us—as he convinced Eve in the garden—that God's way is not best for us, that He doesn't have our best interests at heart, and that our taking charge of our lives will lead to greater happiness and fulfillment.

Acting in sharp contrast to the sheep robber is the true shepherd of the flock who lays down his life to protect and provide for his sheep. Similarly, in sharp contrast to the wily Satan is Jesus, the Good Shepherd, who has "come that [the sheep] may have life, and that they may have it more abundantly." Jesus, the Son of our Creator God, understands why we were created, and He wants what is best for us. Life abundant comes when we walk in God's ways and in close fellowship with Him.

May we journey through life with our Good Shepherd always as our guide.

Lord Jesus, I see the truth so clearly when You talk about sheep, robbers, and the real shepherd. Of course, the shepherd knows what is best for the sheep! Help me see that this truth applies to You, the Good Shepherd, and me, a sheep who would get into trouble without Your protection and guidance. Help me choose to walk in Your ways and in close fellowship with You.

WE CANNOT BE SEPARATED
FROM GOD'S LOVE.

ROMANS 8:38–39

I am persuaded that
neither death nor
life, nor angels nor
principalities nor
powers, nor things
present nor things to
come, nor height nor
depth, nor any other
created thing, shall be
able to separate us from
the love of God which is
in Christ Jesus our Lord.

Feelings lie. Read that fact again: feelings lie.

We can feel that God is far away and that He isn't hearing our prayers. We can feel ignored, forgotten, and unloved by Him. But—again—feelings lie.

Feelings don't necessarily correspond with reality. After all, they are influenced by sleep or the lack thereof; food or the lack thereof; and hormones or their abundance. The checker at the grocery store who snaps at us or the gas attendant who unexpectedly pumps our gas at the self-serve station—both can influence our feelings and our mood.

Feelings of being abandoned by God and the resulting discouragement can lead us to dangerous places. One of the most dangerous places is where we feel distanced or separated from God's love. Feeling that we've lost that mooring can be costly when the storms of life rage. Panic doesn't make for wise and careful navigation through the rocks when the waves come crashing down.

Yes, feelings lie, and they can have a destructive ripple effect in a believer's life. So don't give your feelings a foothold. When your emotions raise their voices, counter that noise with God's truth. Speak His Word out loud. Try doing so using today's verses from Romans 8. No matter how the enemy protests, stand strong in God's truth. It may not take too many minutes or too many verses before God says, "Enough!" And at that point, when at His prompting you say no to deceptive feelings, you are at a place where you will definitely feel His love.

Your Word is the bread of life. Your Word is a lamp unto my feet as it guides me through the rough terrain of life. Your Word is a mirror that shows me my sin. And Your Word is unshakable truth that can make false feelings flee. I thank You, Father God, for this solid foundation for my life—and please help me live in a way that honors and glorifies You.

HEBREWS 10:24–25

Let us consider one another in order to stir up love and good works, not forsaking the assembling of ourselves together, as is the manner of some, but exhorting one another, and so much the more as you see the Day approaching.

GOD DESIGNED COMMUNITY TO GLORIFY HIM AND TO GROW YOU.

It has been said that the last decision we make independently is to become a Christian, because when God calls us to follow Jesus, He calls us to community. We experience that community if we regularly worship at the same church, if we are involved in a small group, and if we attend a weekly Bible study. Ideally, we also experience community with fellow believers when we share the everyday aspects of life—eating meals, shopping, exercising, vacationing, and especially praying.

The writer of Hebrews knew the value of Christian community. He understood that we need one another to spur us on to "love and good works." He realized the value of meeting together regularly and of holding one another accountable. We may know, understand, and realize these truths, but putting them into practice may be tough. *I'm busy. I'm just more of a private person. I've never done well in groups.* And, if we were honest, *It's easier to be anonymous at church* and *I don't like getting close to people.*

Donald Miller, the author of *Blue Like Jazz*, shares what his friend taught him about the value of community: "Rick told me . . . I should be living in community. He said I should have people around bugging me and getting under my skin because without people I could not grow—I could not grow in God, and I could not grow as a human. . . . God wants us together, living among one another, not hiding ourselves under logs like fungus. You are not a fungus, he told me, you are a human, and you need other people in your life in order to be healthy."[32]

Who can argue?

Father God, show me where I am hiding. Maybe I'm not even in relationships the way You want me to be. Or maybe I'm only going through the motions in the fellowship groups I do participate in. Either way, teach me to be honest and genuine in all of my relationships—and change my heart so that I even learn to like it!

DANIEL 3:17-18

If we are thrown into the blazing furnace, the God we serve is able to save us from it, and he will rescue us from your hand, O king. But even if he does not, we want you to know, O king, that we will not serve your gods or worship the image of gold you have set up. (NIV)

CHOOSE TO STAY FAITHFUL,

EVEN THROUGH THE FIRE.

They had been warned. Shadrach, Meshach, and Abednego knew the consequences of not bowing before the golden statue of King Nebuchadnezzar. The edict had been clear: "Whoever does not fall down and worship shall be cast immediately into the midst of a burning fiery furnace" (Daniel 3:6).

Choosing to remain faithful to the God of Abraham, Isaac, and Jacob, these three young men did not deny their disobedience when Nebuchadnezzar summoned them and gave them another chance to worship the statue. Neither did they waver in their loyalty to the God of Israel. Instead, they boldly declared their confidence that God could deliver them from the fiery furnace—and then just as boldly they declared that they would not stop serving Him even if He didn't.

"Even if He doesn't" faith recognizes God's authority and willingly submits to it. It's a faith that trusts God even though the next step looks painful or dangerous, if not deadly. It's a faith that gets the attention of people around us, strengthening believers and often piquing the interest of nonbelievers.

What current situation in your life is an opportunity for "even if He doesn't" faith? In what circumstances can you choose to stay faithful to God, knowing that He may not take the course of action you'd like Him to? Perhaps every occasion to trust God is an opportunity for "even if He doesn't" faith.

So trust. Obey. And watch your Father work in your life and in those around you.

Lord, thank You for the example of Shadrach, Meshach, and Abednego, who were willing to remain faithful to You, whether or not You delivered them from the fiery furnace. Please grow in me that kind of loyalty and faith. May I not waver in my commitment to You, no matter the consequences, and may I have faith that Your plans for me are always best.

---

1 CORINTHIANS 15:58

Therefore, my beloved brethren, be steadfast, immovable, always abounding in the work of the Lord, knowing that your labor is not in vain in the Lord.

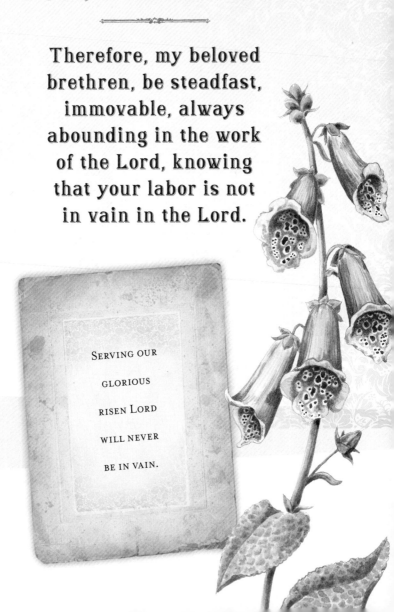

SERVING OUR

GLORIOUS

RISEN LORD

WILL NEVER

BE IN VAIN.

Maybe you've heard this tip for better understanding God's Word: when you hear the word *therefore*, figure out what it's there for! First Corinthians 15:58 is a great example of the effectiveness of this Bible study tool.

Why can believers "be steadfast, immovable, always abounding in the work of the Lord, knowing that your labor is not in vain in the Lord"? Verse 57 is very clear: because God "gives us the victory through our Lord Jesus Christ."

In His resurrection from the dead, Jesus showed His power over sin and death. Victorious over these enemies of ours, Jesus enabled us, who were once dead in our sin, to be in relationship with our holy God and to enjoy fellowship with the risen Lord. Jesus also opened the gates to eternity for those of us who recognize Him as King.

The winds of oppression in this world, peer pressure, chronic illness, persistent physical pain, broken relationships, pressing decisions, stress, exhaustion—so much can weaken our stand in the Lord. We can too easily feel that following Jesus is futile (it can look awfully crazy to the world) and that our kingdom work is pointless (it tends not to bear the concrete, worldly, and satisfying fruit of power, possessions, and prestige).

When such feelings arise, we need only look to the empty tomb. It helps us remember the big-picture perspective we need when we're weighed down here on earth: Jesus rose from the dead, He was victorious over sin, and serving our glorious risen Lord will never be in vain.

How Your truth encourages me! I feel understood: You know I can be shaken by events and opinions, and You know I can feel like my service to You is futile. I feel cared for: You remind me that I'm not alone on this earth. Your Spirit with me and within me enables me to be steadfast and immovable in my faith. May I never lose sight of that truth; may I persevere in doing Your kingdom work.

PSALM 17:7–8

Show Your marvelous
   lovingkindness by
   Your right hand,
O You who save those who
   trust in You
From those who rise up
   against them.
Keep me as the apple of
   Your eye;
Hide me under the shadow
   of Your wings.

YOUR HEAVENLY FATHER WILL ALWAYS

PROTECT YOU AND LOVE YOU.

As if we don't have enough trouble getting along with one another, we also have to deal with diseases, aging, and natural disasters. We face challenges in the marketplace, and we have no control over international trade. And those are only some of the struggles we see.

The apostle Paul reminded us that "we do not wrestle against flesh and blood, but against principalities, against powers, against the rulers of the darkness of this age, against spiritual hosts of wickedness in the heavenly places" (Ephesians 6:12). Thankfully, we have somewhere to go when life gets hard. Psalm 17:7–8 contains some wonderful promises, and those promises become more meaningful upon closer examination.

First, what does it mean to be the apple of the Almighty's eye? One explanation is that the apple refers to the pupil of the human eye, so this expression means that the Lord protects you just as He would instinctively protect that vital organ of vision. Another explanation is that your loving God allows you to get close enough to Him that your image is reflected in the iris of His eye. Whichever explanation you prefer, the bottom line is that God loves you.

Second, "the shadow of Your wings" refers to a mother hen as she spreads out her wings to provide refuge and safety for her chicks. The babies run to the wings of their mother for protection, warmth, and love. We who are God's children are to run to Him for those same reasons.[33]

Whatever comes our way in the world, we can be confident that our heavenly Father will always offer us safety and love.

Father God, I am blessed that You regard me as the apple of Your eye, cherished and precious to You. I thank You that You spread Your wings to provide me a safe refuge. Trusting that You will always protect me, may I never hesitate to run to You when life is dangerous, difficult, or lonely. Thank You for Your unending love.

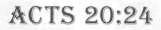

ACTS 20:24

But none of these
things move me;
nor do I count
my life dear to
myself, so that
I may finish my
race with joy,
and the ministry
which I received
from the Lord
Jesus, to testify
to the gospel of
the grace of God.

MAY WE, LIKE PAUL,

RUN OUR EARTHLY

RACE WITH JOY.

The apostle Paul dearly loved the elders of the Ephesian church, and when he visited them on his way to Jerusalem, he wasn't sure if he would ever see them again . . . this side of heaven. Before he exhorted the elders "to shepherd the church of God which He purchased with His own blood" (Acts 20:28) and prayed with them, Paul acknowledged the risks inherent in his trip to Jerusalem. All he knew, he reported, was "that the Holy Spirit testifies . . . saying that chains and tribulations await me" (verse 23).

Then came Paul's bold proclamation in verse 24: those dangers and risks were not going to keep him from going to Jerusalem. What mattered most to Paul was not how long his life lasted, but that—however many days God gave him—he would "finish [his] race with joy."

Paul was confident that the Lord had called him "to testify to the gospel of the grace of God," and he had faithfully fulfilled that calling, often at great cost to his physical health and safety. He was persecuted, and he suffered greatly for the sake of the gospel. And he was willing to suffer some more.

What an example for us! May we, like Paul, finish our earthly race with joy! May we continue to proclaim the gospel with our attitudes, our actions, and our words. May we tell the story of God's grace, made available to us through Jesus' death and resurrection.

When life beats us down and we need to remind ourselves of what really matters, Acts 20:24 is a good place to go.

Lord God, I am so thankful that You not only tell us how to live a life that glorifies You but also give us real-life examples like the apostle Paul. Help me serve You with the kind of commitment and focus he had. Enable me to follow You whatever the cost. Give me bold words when I have the opportunity to share the gospel. And may I, like Paul, run and ultimately finish the race with joy.

JOHN 16:23

Most assuredly, I say to you, whatever you ask the Father in My name He will give you.

IF YOU PRAY IN CHRIST'S NAME, EXPECT THE FATHER TO RESPOND.

Prayer is an amazing privilege and, at times, a perplexing mystery. That the Creator of the universe, the Author of history, would want to have an ongoing conversation with us is an astounding fact. That the sovereign King invites us to ask Him for whatever is on our hearts is a humbling and wonderful truth. That He doesn't always answer our prayers as we ask or according to our timetable can be more than a little discouraging. Some wise believers say that in those situations God is answering with either a "no" or a "not yet," but when we're asking for something that we are confident is His will—saving a soul, healing a marriage—why would He wait? Well, we don't want a God we can totally understand. He wouldn't be very big.

One important teaching about prayer is Jesus' instruction to pray to God in His name. Writer and prayer warrior Stormie Omartian says this: "Praying in the name of Jesus gives us authority over the enemy and proves we have faith in God to do what His Word promises. God knows our thoughts and our needs, but He responds to our prayers. That's because He always gives us a choice about everything, including whether we will trust Him and obey by praying in Jesus' name."[34]

The name Jesus is not a magical abracadabra, just as God Himself is not some genie in a bottle, waiting to grant us whatever we request. When we pray in the name *Jesus*, however, we remember that we are able to approach God only because of Jesus and His spilled blood. We also remember that God is God, and we're not. Thy will be done, Father.

Lord, I often take for granted the privilege of prayer. I too often forget to thank You for Your answers. And there are times when I glibly say, "I'll pray for you," but I don't. Forgive me for treating prayer so lightly, and work in my heart to make me a person who prays passionately, regularly, confidently, and always in the name of Jesus. Grow in me a love for conversing with You. I pray in Jesus' name, amen.

MUNDANE TASKS ARE SIGNIFICANT WHEN WE DO EACH ONE *WITH* AND *FOR* THE LORD.

COLOSSIANS 3:23

Whatever you do, do your work heartily, as for the Lord rather than for men. (NASB)

Face it. Doing laundry and getting the oil changed are simply not glamorous activities. Washing dishes, changing diapers, and clocking in for an 8:00–5:00 job are not at all glitzy. Yet any of these mundane tasks is redeemed and made significant when we do each one *with* and *for* the Lord.

That's the wisdom of Colossians 3:23—"Whatever you do, do your work heartily, as for the Lord rather than for men." That's also the example of the seventeenth-century monk Brother Lawrence, known for his book *The Practice of the Presence of God.* Lawrence not only prayed in chapel at appointed hours, but he also prayed in between as he did the ordinary chores of daily life. "Whether slicing bread, peeling potatoes or washing dishes [Lawrence] did whatever he was doing for the love of God. He did what he was doing as [if] God [were] right next to him doing whatever it was with him. He practiced the presence of God. . . . His practice was to establish himself in a sense of God's presence by continually conversing with God."

What would it be like to drive carpool, run the department, volunteer in the classroom, or make rounds at the hospital with a keen awareness of God's presence? Remember what Brother Lawrence realized: "The topic was not the essential element; the conversation partner was the crucial ingredient. . . . No task was too small or too mundane to do with God. In fact any task, even loading the dishwasher, is an occasion to practice the presence of God."[35]

When we do the tasks at hand in conversation with the Lord, our work becomes worship.

Lord God, teach me to walk through each day very aware that You are with me, and may that awareness lead me to do whatever task is at hand with You and for You. Teach me to enjoy an ongoing conversation with You throughout my days so that I may be sensitive to Your guidance and empowered by Your strength and love.

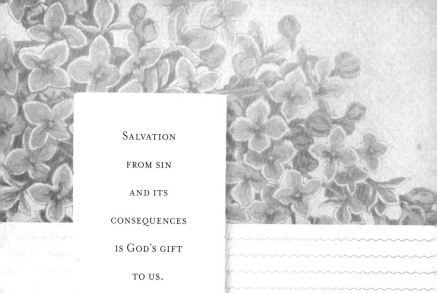

SALVATION

FROM SIN

AND ITS

CONSEQUENCES

IS GOD'S GIFT

TO US.

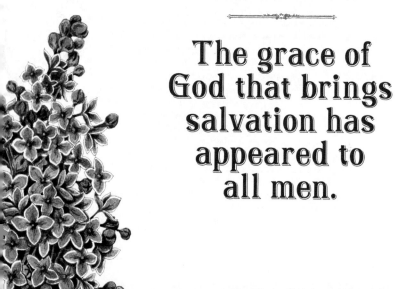

TITUS 2:11

The grace of
God that brings
salvation has
appeared to
all men.

Just show me what to do! Point me in the right direction! How high do you want me to jump? Do you grade on a curve? How many hoops do I need to jump through? Do you give extra credit?

We may not always like the results of systems like these, but at least they make sense to us. We understand about earning the positives and deserving the negatives. Consequences—good and bad—match our actions, good and bad.

God's economy is very different. Oh, He shows us what to do, and He points us in the right direction. He gave us His Law as well as the example of His Son, who lived out that Law perfectly. For the rest of us, however, the Law showed us how far short of God's standards we fell—and would always fall. In other words, the Law revealed our sinfulness to us. We also learned that there is nothing we can do to get rid of that sinfulness.

Enter God's grace! Salvation from sin and its consequences—death and eternal separation from God—is a gift from Him to us sinners. Pure gift. And that can be unsettling.

In *Friendship for Grown-Ups*, Lisa Whelchel puts it this way: "Grace felt too good to be true. I was afraid to trust it. I felt comfortable with the Law. Just tell me what to do so I can do it right and earn love and acceptance. Grace felt all backwards to me. Tell me what to do so I can do it wrong and realize I can't earn love but I can accept it."[36]

And Jesus gave His life in hopes that you will too.

Lord God, You already know this, but it's a whole lot more comfortable for me to earn something than just to be given that something. Especially when that something is immeasurably and indescribably valuable. Especially when that something is forgiveness of my sin and eternal life with You. I am humbled by Your grace. Help me accept Your love—even if it makes me squirm a bit—and then share that love with others, that they may also come to know You and Your grace.

MATTHEW 5:14–15

You are the light of
the world. A city that
is set on a hill cannot
be hidden. Nor do they
light a lamp and put
it under a basket, but
on a lampstand, and it
gives light to all who
are in the house.

GOD'S PEOPLE CAN

LIGHT THE PATH

OUT OF DARKNESS.

It has been said that a picture is worth a thousand words. A picture painted with words—especially one painted by Jesus Himself—can be just as effective.

In Matthew 5, Jesus talked about the role His people play in a world darkened by sin and populated by lost souls. The word picture is simple: "You are the light of the world." God has us in our neighborhoods, schools, workplaces, sports teams, community activities, and even churches to be His light. People in the dark—in spiritual, emotional, or psychological darkness—need light if they are ever to find their way out. That's the role God's people play: we can light the path out of darkness, the path to the hope and wholeness Jesus offers. Even people who are already following God, members of your church, can be encouraged by your light and reminded of the path God wants them to walk.

We will be less than effective—and perhaps totally ineffective—if we hide that light of Christ that is within us. Maybe we're not sure we can defend our faith if someone asks, or we're nervous because we are in the minority on the job or the PTA board. We may simply be hungry for acceptance and desperate to fit in with the crowd. Thoughts like these—planted by the enemy—give us reasons to withdraw, and if we're letting them affect our behavior, we may be hiding our light.

Finally, if His listeners don't quite understand Jesus' word picture, He makes His point crystal clear: "Let your light so shine before men, that they may see your good works and glorify your Father in heaven" (verse 16). Amen!

Lord Jesus, thank You for this word picture and this reminder of how You can use us to have an impact on people lost in darkness. I think of the fact that a little bit of light can affect a huge and very dark room: striking a match in the corner changes the darkness throughout. May that picture as well as Your call to "shine before men" encourage me to shine for You.

PHILIPPIANS 4:11

I have learned in whatever state I am, to be content.

WE DO HAVE A CHOICE IN

OUR OUTLOOK ON LIFE.

Is your glass half empty or half full? Maybe you are a bit of an Eeyore, and your glass is half empty—and you know evaporation, leaks, and getting knocked over will soon mean a completely empty glass. Or maybe you are something of a Pollyanna, and of course your glass is half full—and you're sure it will be overflowing tomorrow!

Whatever bent your personality naturally takes, you do have a choice in your outlook on life. Maybe the Pollyannas among us don't need the lesson that Paul talked about in Philippians 4, but listen up, Eeyores! You may be melancholy by nature: that's how God made you, you say. That doesn't mean you can't reflect a bit of Christian joy and hope as you live your life.

Yes, the world has come a long way—all of it downhill—since Eden. Yes, the human race is living with wrong priorities. But you know the Author of history! You know who wins in the end! You know that Jesus will return victorious over sin and death! Any one of those truths is a reason to smile.

Paul learned to be content whatever his circumstances, and Paul knew very difficult circumstances (see 2 Corinthians 11:23–27). Perhaps knowing that Jesus is indeed the ultimate Victor in the world's battle between evil and good helped Paul. Or maybe he chose to focus on the truth that God is sovereign or that nothing could separate Paul from God's love. Or perhaps Paul was blessed with the Spirit's peace that passes understanding, so contentment was an easy choice.

Pick whatever truth will help you, and teach yourself to choose to be content.

God, keeping my eyes on You and my heart open to Your presence will help me choose contentment, whatever my circumstances. Please help me live in light of this truth. Help me choose to stay grounded in Your sovereignty, Your victory, and Your unfailing love for me. May my circumstances pale in comparison to these glorious truths!

GALATIANS 4:4–7

When the fullness of the time
had come, God sent forth His
Son, born of a woman, born
under the law, to redeem those
who were under the law, that we
might receive the adoption as
sons. And because you are sons,
God has sent forth the Spirit of
His Son into your hearts, crying
out, "Abba, Father!" Therefore
you are no longer a slave but
a son, and if a son, then an
heir of God through Christ.

NO LONGER SLAVES,

WE HAVE BEEN

ADOPTED AS SONS.

It's a sad truth about human nature that we can become blind, deaf, and numb to the wonders around us. We forget that the child in our arms is an unspeakable miracle, as are the rosebushes blooming in the garden, the movement of the planets in their orbits, and our ability to think, feel, and communicate. We are deaf to the proclamation of God's majesty that can be heard in the roaring ocean and starry skies. And, saddest of all, the gospel can become so familiar that we don't hear it anymore for the amazing grace of God that it reveals.

So take time right now to read again—and to read slowly—Paul's words in Galatians 4:4–7. Note the wondrous truths that you may have heard hundreds of times. God's Son was "born of a woman." God's plan of salvation includes our "adoption as sons." We are privileged to call the almighty Creator and Sustainer of life "Daddy, Abba." And we receive these blessings—and many others—through Christ who died as payment for our sins.

Knowing this gospel truth is a blessing in itself—and we are called to share this blessed knowledge with others (Matthew 28:18–20). Are you ready and able to do so? Do you know what you would say to someone who wants to know the reason for the hope that is within you (1 Peter 3:15)? What would you say about your own journey of faith and the difference that knowing Jesus has made in your life? By the power of the Holy Spirit within you, your own story will make the gospel truths of Galatians 4 come alive.

Thank You that You have called me to know the truth of the gospel—and thank You for the difference You make in my life. Lord God, I have hope and peace in You. You have given my life purpose and meaning. I know the power of the Holy Spirit and the comfort of Your love. Your Word is the light for my path. Enable me, I ask, to share clearly and boldly about my relationship with You whenever I have the opportunity.

REVELATION 4:11

You are worthy, O Lord,
To receive glory and honor and power;
For You created all things,
And by Your will they exist
and were created.

GOD ALONE
DESERVES OUR
SONGS OF GLORY,
HONOR, AND
POWER.

The setting is the throne room of heaven. A rainbow encircles the throne, and sitting on it is One who "was like a jasper and a sardius stone in appearance" (Revelation 4:3). The jasper probably refers to a diamond that "refracts all the colors of the spectrum in wondrous brilliance"; the sardius was a fiery bright ruby red stone; and the rainbow surrounding the throne was dominated by an emerald-green tone.[37] Twenty-four elders, each on a throne, are wearing radiant white robes and golden crowns. Thunder and lightning come forth from the throne, and lamps of fire burn in front of it.

Four mysterious living creatures—resembling a lion, a calf, a man, and a flying eagle—sing their own song of worship: "Holy, holy, holy, Lord God Almighty, who was and is and is to come!" (verse 8). Their chorus of praise prompts the twenty-four elders to fall down before the One sitting on the throne and worship Him in all His majesty. Their words resound in the throne room, declaring the worthiness of the Sovereign and Holy One. He created all things, He sustains His creation, and He alone deserves glory, honor, and power.

Revelation 4 offers a scene in the future, but the world we live in has its own ways of bringing forth our adoration and worship. What in the physical world offers you hints of God's majesty? What reveals to you something of His infinite power? Where do you see evidence that He is sustaining His creation? And what does your song of praise sound like? The Lord truly is worthy of all your praise!

All power is Yours! All glory is Yours! All honor is due Your name! You created us to praise You, and I do that now, almighty God. Great are the works of Your hands! Great is Your faithfulness to me! Your truth guides me, Your Word sustains me, and Your grace is amazing. I am humbled by Your sacrificial and unconditional love for me. Truly, You alone are worthy of praise.

1 CORINTHIANS 6:19

Do you not know that your body is the temple of the Holy Spirit who is in you, whom you have from God, and you are not your own?

YOUR BODY IS A
SANCTUARY WHERE
GOD DWELLS.

Eat this! Don't eat that! Wear this! Don't wear that! Exercise like this! Work out this long and this often! Take this supplement! Try this makeup! We can get lots of input from many sources about how to take care of our bodies. In 1 Corinthians 6:19, though, the apostle Paul set forth the solid bottom line for each one of us.

Your body is "the temple of the Holy Spirit," he wrote, and the Greek word he used in this context is very significant. Rather than using *hieron* to refer to the entire temple complex, Paul used the word *naos* to refer to a specific part of the temple complex. Paul was telling believers then and now that our bodies were a sanctuary for God. Just as the glory of God filled the temple in 1 Kings 8:10–11, "now the glory of God in the person of the Holy Spirit dwells within every believer."[38]

Think about that for a minute. Your body is a sanctuary where God dwells. The all holy, almighty God has chosen to take up residence within you to guide you, grow you, and bless you. What are the implications of your body being a dwelling place of the Holy One? As you think about that question, consider specifically which behaviors or attitudes you could and perhaps should purge from your heart and your life. What activities should you stop doing—and what activities should you start doing? Are your clothes appropriate? Your makeup? And are you exercising often enough and hard enough? And what about your diet?

Care for your body, for your own sake and because it is the dwelling place of God.

Holy Spirit, it is truly amazing that You dwell within me. May I make choices about how I live—how I care for my heart, my soul, my body—based on that fact. You, Lord, deserve the best of dwelling places. Help me strive for a healthy body so that I can better enjoy Your presence within me every moment of my life.

PSALM 139:23-24

Search me, O God, and know my heart;
Try me, and know my anxieties;
And see if there is any wicked way in me,
And lead me in the way everlasting.

GOD CALLS US TO

CONFESSION AND BRINGS

HEALING TO OUR SOUL.

You've probably heard it said that confession is good for the soul. Perhaps you've even experienced the relief that comes with confessing your sin to your holy God. He is indeed faithful and just to forgive you when you acknowledge your sin before Him (1 John 1:9). Perhaps you've also experienced the relief that comes with confessing your sin to a sister or brother in the Lord (James 5:16)—and the response was a taste of God's unconditional love for you, whether in the form of tears of compassion, prayer, a hug, or something else. God calls us to confession because it brings healing to our relationship with Him and to our soul.

Sometimes, though, we are blind to our sin or so comfortable with a particular behavior or attitude that we don't recognize it as sin. This reality prompted David's prayer in Psalm 139:23–24. Asking for God's help in identifying his sinful ways was a key step toward experiencing the Lord's forgiveness and renewed fellowship with Him.

As crucial as confession is to our walk with the Lord, consider what author Peter De Vries has said: "Confession is good for the soul only in the sense that a tweed coat is good for dandruff—it is a palliative rather than a remedy."[39] Confession does ease the burden from our soul and bridge the distance between us and God. But the actual remedy for our sin was Jesus' death: He died in our place so that we may be considered righteous in God's sight.

So regularly confess your sin, and when you do, look at the cross. Jesus' death there was the costly remedy for that sin.

Almighty God, Your plan of grace is beautiful in its coherence and freeing with its invitation to be a member of Your eternal family. Thank You that Your Holy Spirit continues to work in my heart to reveal my sin so that I may confess all that interferes with my fellowship with You. And, most of all, thank You for sending Your Son to die as payment and remedy for my sin.

EPHESIANS 3:17–21

May [Christ] dwell in your hearts through faith;
that you, being rooted and grounded in love,
may be able to comprehend with all the saints
what is the width and length and depth and
height—to know the love of Christ which passes
knowledge; that you may be filled with all the
fullness of God. Now to Him who is able to do
exceedingly abundantly above all that we ask or
think, according to the power that works in us,
to Him be glory in the church by Christ Jesus
to all generations, forever and ever. Amen.

MAY PEOPLE WE LOVE
KNOW MORE FULLY HOW
MUCH GOD LOVES THEM.

During His earthly ministry, Jesus taught His followers, then and now, to persevere in prayer, to be specific with our requests, and to always submit to God's will when we pray. Our heavenly Father cares about the details of our lives just as earthly fathers care about the details of their children's lives. We are commanded to cast all our worries on the Lord (1 Peter 5:7), and we can be sure that He will provide for our needs (Matthew 6:31–32).

That said, we nevertheless need to pray for far more than just the details of everyday life, more than even the tough, painful circumstances we and those we love find ourselves in. We need to pray with the big-picture, eternal perspective in mind: we need to pray for spiritual health and growth for those people we care about, for the children we influence, and for ourselves.

After all, God's love is wider, longer, deeper, and higher than any of us can fully comprehend this side of heaven. God's love for us "passes knowledge," yet our greater knowledge of that love is an indescribably worthwhile, lifelong pursuit. So among the life-giving—and the eternal life-giving—prayers we can offer on behalf of others, this desire that they would know more fully how much God loves them is paramount.

And when we pray, we do well to remember that the One to whom we are praying is "able to do exceedingly abundantly above all that we ask or think." So may we pray confidently, joyfully, and consistently for greater knowledge of God's great love for us, His children—and then be amazed by how He answers!

Lord God, it is easy to be focused on the details and demands of everyday life. Thank You for this passage from Ephesians that reminds me of some key reasons to pray. Even as I pray for specific requests, may I also pray for those people to grow in their knowledge of how much You love them. And may I also come to know more completely the width, length, depth, and height of Your love for me.

ROMANS 12:1

I beseech you
therefore, brethren,
by the mercies
of God, that you
present your bodies
a living sacrifice,
holy, acceptable to
God, which is your
reasonable service.

WE ARE TO

DIE TO SELF.

What do you think of when you hear the word *sacrifice*? What scenes from the Bible come to mind?

The Genesis 22 account of Abraham and Isaac is one of the most well-known Old Testament stories. God commanded Abraham to sacrifice his long-awaited firstborn son, the son through whom God had promised to bless the world. As remarkable as it sounds, Abraham appears to have obeyed without hesitation—and God provided a replacement sacrifice just moments before Abraham was to kill his only son.

The New Testament accounts of Jesus dying on the cross offer another story of sacrifice, but this time God did not provide a replacement. He allowed His only Son to be killed, to die an excruciatingly painful death on a Roman cross—and Jesus submitted to that plan.

Then comes from Paul the command that we who name the resurrected Jesus our Savior and Lord are to "present [our] bodies a living sacrifice." We are to die to self—to our sinful desires, to our corrupt self-will, and to dreams that are not in line with God's plans. By the power of God's Spirit, we are to obey His commands rather than let the world shape us. We are to submit to God's will in all we do, just as Jesus submitted to God's will on Calvary, and ours is not a once-and-for-all act.

Here's how pastor David Jeremiah put it: "Living sacrifices don't die physically, but they must die spiritually every day. As someone has well said, 'The problem with living sacrifices is they keep crawling off the altar.' Look around—if you're standing on the ground, it's time to get back on the altar."[40]

Lord, please show me the ways I have crawled off the altar. Help me see myself honestly. Please reveal selfishness, deliberate disobedience, and even the unconscious ways I automatically defer to my own will and wishes. I know that life works better when I live it according to Your will. Please empower me by Your Spirit to do exactly that.

1 CHRONICLES 28:9

As for you, my son Solomon, know the God of your father, and serve Him with a loyal heart and with a willing mind; for the Lord searches all hearts and understands all the intent of the thoughts. If you seek Him, He will be found by you; but if you forsake Him, He will cast you off forever.

LOYAL SERVANTS WHO SEEK THE LORD WILL ALWAYS FIND HIM.

Father knows best, but will the children listen?

Near the close of David's reign, he did what any dad would do. David had announced to the nation of Israel that God had chosen his son Solomon to be their next king and that Solomon would have the privilege of building the temple. But before handing over the scepter, David had a few thoughts to share. Coming from someone blessed to be called a man after God's own heart (see 1 Samuel 13:14), his words just may have been worth listening to. After all, David had done what Solomon was soon to do. David knew the demands, the pressures, the temptations, and the responsibilities of the kingship. And he had learned some life lessons the hard way.

David had often sought the Lord for guidance and direction, but at other times he had made his own plans, gone his own way, and paid the price. Having hidden God's Word in his heart (Psalm 119:11), David knew God's commands and obeyed them. But, as someone has commented, on at least one occasion God's truth was hidden so deeply in David's heart that he apparently misplaced it! David sinned greatly, and when he confessed, he eloquently celebrated God's forgiveness (Psalm 51).

David understood the importance of knowing God, of serving Him with a loyal heart and a willing mind, and of seeking Him persistently until you find Him. David also knew that forsaking God comes with a huge cost.

Father knows best, but will we listen? May we learn from these lessons that David learned the hard way!

Help me, Lord God, to learn from what David told Solomon. Even more importantly, please help me live out those truths. May I be disciplined in my efforts to know You better, loyal and willing to serve You, diligent in both seeking You and obeying You, and faithful to You so that You will never have reason to cast me off. And keep me, I pray, from ever forsaking You.

LAMENTATIONS 3:22-23

Through the LORD's mercies we are not consumed,
  Because His compassions fail not.
They are new every morning;
  Great is Your faithfulness.

IN GOD ALONE

DO WE FIND

TRUE PROVISION

FOR EACH DAY.

How do people read the paper without becoming utterly depressed by the evil, the injustice, and the sheer magnitude of the economic, social, and international problems that make the news? How do parents let children out of their sight if they aren't entrusting them to the Lord's care? "Hope it all works out for you" seems like an unfinished thought, and "Just have faith!" seems to be an incomplete instruction.

Why get up in the morning? What is the basis for anything you teach your kids? Hope in what? Faith in whom? The world must be a frightening place for those who don't know the Lord, the Designer of the universe, the Author of history, and the Victor over sin and death. This all-powerful, all-knowing God, however, is not some distant, impersonal force. Instead, He knows your name, your heart, and your tears. He is merciful, compassionate, and faithful.

In God alone can we find genuine hope for the circumstances of the world and the future of our kids. Hope that is not rooted in Him is not much more than wishful thinking, and faith in anything or anyone else is utterly without foundation.

Anne Jackson, the author of *Permission to Speak Freely*, knows this God well: "There is a light at the end of the tunnel. There is a God who is faithful to give you exactly what you need. Whatever it is. He'll provide what you need, when you can't handle things anymore. Whatever happens may not look like what you expect or come at a time when you think you need it most, but in the end, I promise you—I confess to you—He's faithful."[41]

Where else, Lord God, can I turn for hope except to You? You alone offer security for the future as well as for the present. You alone keep every promise You make—every promise of protection, of provision, and of Your presence with me. Teach me, Father, to rest in Your loving plan for me, to keep my eyes on Jesus, and to rejoice in the hope I have in Him alone.

THE HOLY SPIRIT
HELPS US LIVE
ACCORDING TO
JESUS' GOLDEN
RULE.

MATTHEW 7:12

Whatever you want
men to do to you,
do also to them,
for this is the Law
and the Prophets.

It's a basic law of physics. In fact, it's one of Sir Isaac Newton's top three: for every action there is an equal and opposite reaction. Sadly, this principle seems to function in human relationships too. One mean word prompts another mean word. One selfish act invites a selfish act in return. One cruel stare receives a cruel glare in response. And it's a frightening fact that the second mean word, the second selfish act, and the second cruel stare are usually not premeditated. We simply react!

Reacting instead of thinking about our responses to people—to their kind or their mean words, to their selfless or selfish acts, to their compassionate or cruel glances—is our usual way of behaving. Since we were young, we've been told to think before we speak, and we're still working on it! We've probably also been working on not retaliating when someone hurts us, but an eye for an eye comes much more easily than turning the other cheek.

Only with the Holy Spirit's intervention can we stop responding to people in our natural eye-for-an-eye way. The Spirit's work in our hearts bears the fruit of "love, joy, peace, longsuffering, kindness, goodness, faithfulness, gentleness, self-control" (Galatians 5:22–23). This fruit of transformation will help us do a better job of returning a kind word for a mean one, an unselfish act for a selfish one, and a look of compassion for a cruel glare. In other words, one result of the Holy Spirit's work in our hearts will be an easier adherence to the Golden Rule. The Spirit will enable us to treat others the way we ourselves want to be treated.

Father God, I much more quickly react in kind rather than treating people the way I want to be treated. Please forgive me, and, Holy Spirit, please continue to do Your transforming work in me. I want to be able to love with God's love and treat people according to the Golden Rule. And I definitely need Your help.

PHILIPPIANS 1:6

Being confident of
this very thing, that
He who has begun a
good work in you will
complete it until the
day of Jesus Christ.

GOD WILL NOT

LET YOU GO.

Do you sometimes have a hard time finishing a project you start? Are you easily discouraged if you encounter unexpected challenges and unanticipated roadblocks? And what if you are part of a team and some members seem to be taking the project two steps backward every time they try to help? Fortunately, our heavenly Father is not like that at all.

When God enables us to recognize our sin and our need for forgiveness, He won't stop until He finishes. And He won't consider Himself finished until the final product meets His high standards of purity, holiness, and—in eternity—Christlikeness. Furthermore, God is not surprised by the challenges that come with our lack of cooperation or the roadblocks we erect with our sinful ways and selfish desires. He expects hardened hearts and too busy schedules. He knows we'll make wrong choices and have wrong priorities. Yet God will not let us go.

Singer and songwriter Natalie Grant has learned that lesson and, along the way, this important truth: "A love like [Jesus' love] changes a person. It knows every horrible little secret, every selfish, unkind word and still says, 'I choose you.' It magnifies beauty that has long gone unnoticed, like that of an old painting buried in an attic, worthless and forgotten, until the dust is brushed away and the master artist's signature is revealed, validating the painting's true worth."[42]

The Master Artist's signature reads *Yahweh*, and it's written on your heart, just as your name is written on the palms of His Son's hands. And the Artist who began that good work in you will indeed see it through to completion.

Lord God, help me open my heart to Your life-changing love. I do feel like a dusty old painting: I am too aware of my sinful ways, my selfish plans, my wrong choices, and my skewed priorities. Help me yield to Your efforts to brush away the dust. May I be clay in Your hands as You make me more like Christ. For my good and Your glory!

2 CORINTHIANS 4:16–18

Therefore we do not lose heart. Even though our outward man is perishing, yet the inward man is being renewed day by day. For our light affliction, which is but for a moment, is working for us a far more exceeding and eternal weight of glory, while we do not look at the things which are seen, but at the things which are not seen. For the things which are seen are temporary, but the things which are not seen are eternal.

CHOOSE THE UNSEEN AND ETERNAL
OVER THE SEEN AND TEMPORARY.

No one could convince you that black is white or up is down. But Paul does a good job here of making a case that heavy is light. And it's all a matter of perspective.

A burden is heavy when its presence is pointless, when traveling with it is lonely, and when the journey is long. First, Paul reminded believers that life's afflictions are purposeful, not pointless. God uses our hardships to make us more like Jesus, and no purpose is greater than that. Furthermore, Christlikeness will indeed mean "a far more exceeding and eternal weight of glory" after our days on earth are done.

We need not travel alone during this lifelong process of transformation. Fellow believers have their own afflictions too, and we can be physical reminders for one another that hard times come to believers—that was one of Jesus' promises—but that God is sovereign over even those hard times.

Finally, walking with fellow believers despite the afflictions can make the journey seem shorter. Their companionship can also help us keep focused not on the struggles but on the unseen and eternal rewards that God has for His people.

No pain is wasted in God's economy as He works to transform us. Nothing happens in the lives of God's people without His allowing it in His total sovereignty and perfect wisdom. And no hardship needs to be endured alone. Trust in God's sovereign goodness, walk with His people, and remind yourself that the unseen and eternal are far more important than the seen and temporary. Life's afflictions will then be lighter.

Thank You for Paul's words here, Lord. They are a source of encouragement, based in the truth I know about You and shared by someone who lived out this truth. The contrast between light affliction and eternal weight of glory enables me to put struggles, pain, and hard-to-figure-out situations in Your hands. Thank You that You are sovereign, wise, and good. Thank You for loving me.

HEBREWS 11:1

Now faith is being sure of what we hope for and certain of what we do not see. (NIV)

HOPE IN THE LORD GOD

IS THE ONLY HOPE THAT

WILL NEVER DISAPPOINT.

What are you hoping for? Probably not winning the lottery. Even if you were a gambler, you know the odds are very much against you. Probably not having Prince Charming knock on your door. You know that only happens in fairy tales. And you're probably not hoping for a cure for the common cold to be announced anytime soon. You know that scientists have been trying to nail that virus for years.

In the eighteenth century, Alexander Pope noted that "hope springs eternal in the human breast." That may be so, but whatever we are hoping in will determine whether or not our hope will pay off. Hear what Sheila Walsh wisely says about hope:

> Hope on its own has no power. I can hope to wake up one morning and be three inches taller than the night before, but that hope would not serve me well. Hope depends on what it is linked to. . . . Our hope in Christ is surer than anything we can see and experience on this earth, and we arrive at that place through faith. . . . [Faith] is a commitment to walk in the footsteps of Christ, not knowing what lies ahead, but knowing that He is with us, therefore we can take the next step. Our walk with Christ at times takes us through dark places where it seems as if the sun will never shine again, and we may well feel abandoned. Faith calls us to live above what we feel to what we know to be true.[43]

Hope in anything or anyone other than the Lord may disappoint. Hope that the Lord will bless, now and into eternity, a life of faith in Him is hope that will never disappoint.

Lord God, thank You for the very real hope I have in You. Knowing You in all Your goodness, power, mercy, and love makes the hope I have much more than mere wishful thinking. Hope in You, rooted in Your written Word and in the risen Christ, gives me confidence about life on this earth and about eternal life.

MATTHEW 11:28-30

Come to Me, all you who
labor and are heavy laden,
and I will give you rest.
Take My yoke upon you
and learn from Me, for I
am gentle and lowly in
heart, and you will find
rest for your souls. For
My yoke is easy and
My burden is light.

If you're a parent, don't you wish you could sometimes be told to take a timeout? To go to your room and read a book for twenty minutes? To sit quietly in the corner and think about what just happened? Aaaahhhh . . .

Well, that's the kind of invitation Jesus has extended to you, for the good of your soul, in Matthew 11:28–30. He invites you to go to Him and receive some much needed soul rest.

Consider what burdens are weighing you down. Perhaps you're carrying a burden of sin, of trying to be worthy, or of feeling very much alone in life. Maybe yours is the burden of anxiety, depression, fear, or doubt. The alternative to these burdens is the yoke Jesus offers. And putting on the yoke He has custom-made for you means you have to take off whatever yoke is currently weighing you down.

Taking on the yoke of Christ is choosing to submit to Him, to obey His Word, and to be guided by Him. It is acknowledging His authority over every aspect of your life. Notice that Jesus' invitation to take on His yoke is followed by His promise that "you will find rest." Any guilt caused by sin will be replaced by forgiveness. Peace will replace anxiety; love, fear; joy, depression; and hope, doubt.

The rest Jesus promises is rooted in God's love and forgiveness. The rest He promises is not rest from work; it's not eternal vacation and no more labor. But Jesus' yoke will mean being led to exactly the work and the place God has for you and being led once you're there. So choose to come, choose to take, and find rest for your soul.

Lord, You know the burdens I'm carrying and the reasons for my heavy heart even before I speak them. Thank You that I can leave them at Your feet and take on Your yoke. Father, I long to walk with You, enjoying Your loving presence with me. I feel more at peace just thinking about it.

---

1 CORINTHIANS 10:13

No temptation has overtaken you except such as is common to man; but God is faithful, who will not allow you to be tempted beyond what you are able, but with the temptation will also make the way of escape, that you may be able to bear it.

WHEN TEMPTATION STRIKES, CRY OUT TO GOD FOR HELP.

Maybe you've said with a wry smile, "God won't let us be tempted beyond what we can handle—but I think He has me confused with someone else!"

No chance, but every one of us knows that feeling. Each of us is well aware of the many temptations that fill our world and often fill our days. The apostle Paul certainly did, and this warning to believers in Corinth came after a list of lessons they (and we!) can learn from the children of Israel.

During their forty-year journey between Egypt and Canaan (the 250 miles could have been traveled in a month!), God's people misused their freedom and were tripped up by prideful overconfidence. The behavior that resulted included idolatry, sexual immorality, rebelliousness, testing God, complaining—and we could easily be guilty of the same, if we haven't been already.

So let's—as Paul exhorted—learn from our ancestors in the faith. Let us be firmly rooted in the rich truths of 1 Corinthians 10:13. God is faithful to help us stand strong in the face of temptation. He will not give us an impossible-to-resist temptation, and He will always provide a way of escape. We do, however, need to be mindful of both His presence with us and what He wants to give us when temptations arise. Then we need to be willing to humbly cry out to Him for help.

If there's a verse worth hiding in your heart, it's 1 Corinthians 10:13. Its rich truth will help you live out your faith when temptation strikes—and to live it out for your good and for God's glory.

Lord, I believe that You will help me stand strong when I'm tempted to do something against Your will. I believe that You will not give me an impossible-to-resist temptation. I believe that You will always provide a way of escape. Help my unbelief—and prompt me to humble myself and cry out to You whenever I face temptation and need Your strength and protection.

JUDE 1:24–25

Now to Him who is able
to keep you from stumbling,
And to present you faultless
Before the presence of His glory
with exceeding joy,
To God our Savior,
Who alone is wise,
Be glory and majesty,
Dominion and power,
Both now and forever.
Amen.

GIVE GLORY TO THE

INFINITE GOD WHO

KNOWS YOU BY NAME.

Looking at the multitudes of stars in the sky, staring out at the distant horizon where sky meets ocean, gazing at majestic mountain peaks, listening to crashing thunder—moments like these can remind us of the otherness of our eternal, omnipresent, and infinitely powerful God. He deserves our immeasurable respect and an awe that compels us to fall prostrate before Him. To Him, as Jude declared, "be glory and majesty, dominion and power, both now and forever. Amen."

Yet, sometimes in our mind, God seems to be the gentle grandfather, the buddy and friend, or the generous Santa Claus in the sky. We do ourselves and our relationship with our heavenly Father a great disservice when we lose sight of His awesome otherness and infinite glory. But we don't want to gain that perspective and, at the same time, lose our awareness that He is our personal Savior, Redeemer, heavenly Father, and constant Companion in life.

Singer Natalie Grant says this: "Therein lies the mystery and beauty of the greatness of our God. He is both big and small to us. . . . No sky can contain Him, and no matter how big and grand He is, there's nothing that can separate me from the love of God. . . . God is great enough to be in control of every situation of our life, but small enough to be involved in the smallness of our life. No matter how big He is, God has personal, individual and crafted love for each one of us."[44]

To Him, indeed, be all glory now and forever. Amen!

The world You created offers me vivid reminders of Your immeasurable power and Your essential otherness. The life You have blessed me with—salvation and redemption, family and friends, food and shelter, protection and presence—confirms Your personal love and care. I praise You for the privilege of being in an intimate relationship with You, my infinite God.

JEREMIAH 29:11–13

"For I know the plans I have for you," declares the LORD, "plans to prosper you and not to harm you, plans to give you hope and a future. Then you will call upon me and come and pray to me, and I will listen to you. You will seek me and find me when you seek me with all your heart." (NIV)

SEEK THE LORD, PRAY TO HIM, AND TRUST IN HIS GOOD PLANS FOR YOU.

There's nothing like a flashlight when the power goes out on a dark winter night. There's nothing like a hug when the world seems to have turned against you. And there's nothing like good news when the hurts of the past weigh you down, when the burdens of the present overwhelm, and when the future looks bleak. Today's passage was something like that flashlight, that hug, and that bit of good news for the Jews who were still being held captive in Babylon.

Speaking to His suffering people, God made promises about what would happen once the prophesied seventy years of exile in Babylon were done. He told the struggling people of Israel that He had good plans for them and that they could trust Him to provide them with a wonderful future. And that wonderful future would be a time when God's people would call to Him and He would listen. They would seek Him wholeheartedly, and they would find Him. They would pray to God, and they would trust Him.

Maybe you feel as if you're in a Babylon of your own. Consequences from past decisions are weighing you down, you feel captive to hardships in the present, and you see only darkness ahead. If any of that applies to you, accept God's invitation to you. He will hear your prayers, He will be found by you when you seek Him, and He has wonderful plans for your future.

Move on from past mistakes and missteps. Choose to walk with your Lord today. And look to the future, trusting your good God and the plans He has custom-made for you.

Calling You "Lord" reminds me that You are sovereign. Nothing falls outside Your jurisdiction, and Your power has no limits. You, almighty God, are the Author of history. You oversee the unfolding of world history as well as the unfolding of my own personal history. I praise You that Your plans—for the world at large and for believers like me—are limited only by Your mercy, grace, and love.

PSALM 121

I will lift up my eyes to the hills
   From whence comes my help?
My help comes from the L ORD ,
   Who made heaven and earth.
He will not allow your foot to be moved;
   He who keeps you will not slumber.
Behold, He who keeps Israel
   Shall neither slumber nor sleep.
The L ORD is your keeper;
   The L ORD is your shade at your right hand.
The sun shall not strike you by day,
   Nor the moon by night.
The L ORD shall preserve you from all evil;
   He shall preserve your soul.
The L ORD shall preserve your going out
      and your coming in
   From this time forth,
      and even forevermore.

What wonderful promises in this rich and encouraging psalm! Read it aloud—slower than usual—so you can truly hear its message. Which promise is especially encouraging and significant to you today? Why?

This psalm—one of the seventeen songs or psalms of ascent—was a marching song for faithful Jews making their way to Jerusalem for one of the three yearly feasts. With Jerusalem at an elevation of about 2,700 feet, the ascent was literal, but consider these words of praise. These lines definitely help worshipers ascend figuratively into the presence of the Lord—our keeper, our shade, the preserver of our souls, and our protector along the journey of life.

Reflect for a few minutes on times when you have been very aware of God acting in your life in one or two of the ways these lines describe. When, for instance, has God been your keeper or your shade? When has He clearly preserved you from the evil that flourishes in this fallen world?

As you walk this leg of your life journey, are there times when you feel as if you're truly climbing a mountain? In what ways do you need your Lord to be your shade? From what evil would you like Him to protect you? Know that your heavenly Father is up to the task. An ever-vigilant Shepherd, He never slumbers or sleeps.

> THE LORD IS OUR KEEPER, OUR PROTECTOR, AND THE PRESERVER OF OUR SOULS.

Thank You for the gift of a memory, Lord, so that I can recall Your great faithfulness to me. I am always encouraged when I think back on those times when I, like the psalmist here, was blessed by Your companionship, protection, and guidance. Keep me mindful of—and keep me looking for—ways You shepherd me even now. I do want to enjoy Your company through this journey of life.

JESUS IS SUFFICIENT TO
MEET YOUR EVERY NEED.

PHILIPPIANS 4:13

For I can do everything through Christ, who gives me strength. (NLT)

The list is sobering. Shipwrecked, beaten, imprisoned, stoned, run out of town, hungry, thirsty, cold, naked, threatened by Gentiles and fellow Jews, facing danger in cities, on the sea, and in the wilderness—Paul experienced all of this and more as he served his Lord and Savior. And who saw him through? His Lord and Savior. Each step of the way.

And that's a lesson believers can only learn firsthand. As Bible teacher Beth Moore says, "I can tell you God will meet your every need. I can say that you can do all things through Christ; but until you find out for yourself, it's still a secret. I can tell you, but He will show you. Let Him."[45]

What are you facing right now? Perhaps metaphorically you're dealing with a shipwrecked relationship or a beating in your place of employment. Maybe you feel imprisoned by past sin, unpaid bills, or a meaningless job. The end of a significant relationship may have left you feeling cold and alone. A cross-country move may have left you hungry and thirsty for friends, fellowship, and a church to call home. Life can be very difficult, but hear again the confident statement of the apostle Paul: "I can do everything through Christ, who gives me strength."

As our Savior and our Lord, as our Hope and our Shepherd, Jesus is indeed an unwavering source of strength for us, the most reliable source available to us. He will never leave you or forsake you (see Hebrews 13:5). He will show Himself to be sufficient to meet your every need. As Beth Moore said, give Him the opportunity to do just that.

Lord God, I'm encouraged that the apostle Paul never wavered in his faith in You, and I want to be able to do the same when I feel shipwrecked, beaten down, and threatened. I also appreciate the challenge: how will I know You to be sufficient to meet my every need if I don't have those needs and if I don't turn to You in the midst of them? I believe; help my unbelief—and enable me to trust You more.

MATTHEW 6:9–13

Our Father in heaven,
Hallowed be Your name.
Your kingdom come.
Your will be done
On earth as it is in heaven.
Give us this day our daily bread.
And forgive us our debts,
As we forgive our debtors.
And do not lead us into temptation,
But deliver us from the evil one.
For Yours is the kingdom and the power
and the glory forever. Amen.

Entire books have been written about the Lord's Prayer and complete chapters about a single line. And that isn't too surprising. Of course, we find much to learn here. After all, this example is given to us by the One who lived a life of prayer, whose communion with the Father was unbroken except for the three days after the Crucifixion.

As familiar as this prayer may be to you, try to imagine how radical the first two words—"Our Father"—must have sounded to Jewish ears in the first century. For generations the Almighty's name had been too holy to say out loud. So the drastic shift from a name so holy that no one was allowed to speak it to *Abba*, *Daddy* was truly astounding. Jesus the Son encouraged all believers to approach His heavenly Father as their heavenly Father. The holy God of Israel was welcoming us just like an earthly father drawing his kids into a warm embrace.

But consider what we learn about this Father at the end of the prayer. Not only is He more than able to fulfill each request listed in this passage—and to do so in ways far greater than we could ask or imagine—but He is the ultimate Ruler over all of history and the sovereign King of all creation. So Jesus closed His prayer with words that point to the majesty and otherness of our God: "For Yours is the kingdom and the power and the glory forever." Our warm, caring, heavenly Daddy is at the same time the infinitely powerful King of all creation. And we are privileged to crawl onto His lap and share our hearts.

You are my warm, caring, heavenly Daddy—and, at the same time, the infinite and infinitely powerful King of all creation. Help me keep these two truths in balance so that I will pray not only openly, honestly, and trustingly, but also with respect and a genuine readiness to submit to Your will in all things. What a blessing and a privilege to call You "Daddy"! What a blessing and a privilege to be Your child. And what a blessing of hope and peace to know that Your kingdom, power, and glory are forever!

WORSHIP THE
LORD WITH
GLADNESS!

PSALM 100

Shout for joy to the LORD, all the earth.
Worship the LORD with gladness;
come before him with joyful songs.
Know that the LORD is God.
It is he who made us, and we are his;
we are his people, the sheep of his pasture.
Enter his gates with thanksgiving
and his courts with praise;
give thanks to him and praise his name.
For the LORD is good and his
love endures forever;
his faithfulness continues through
all generations. (NIV)

It's a command made easy to follow. Psalm 100 opens with the call to joyfully praise the Lord and then offers several reasons why we can do exactly that.

The Lord—the One who is stronger than sin and death, the Author of history—is your God. He knows you by name, and He numbers the hair on your head.

This same all-powerful God knit you together in your mother's womb and has planned every day of your life. No matter how often or how far we stray from Him, He still loves us.

God is like a shepherd who, 24/7, protects and provides for His stupid sheep. It's not a flattering description, but like sheep, we find ourselves drawn to unhealthy waters. Sometimes we get ourselves turned upside down and can't get right side up without the Shepherd's help.

Our God is good, not a fearsome figure that idol worshippers have conjured up through the ages. Yahweh wants what is best for us, and He especially desires to have us walk with Him closely every day of our lives.

In sharp contrast to human love that can be fickle, God's love will last forever. He won't change His mind; He won't find someone better to love. And there's nothing you can do to make Him love you less or love you more.

God has been faithful to generations before us, He shows Himself faithful to us, and He will be faithful to every generation to come. Clearly, we have no excuse not to obey the Psalm 100 command! Let us worship the Lord with gladness!

Lord God, the picture of You that Psalm 100 paints is rich in reasons for me to sing Your praises. When I read about the glorious hope I have in You and the intimate care You offer me, I am humbled. I am also encouraged by the bold, confident statements that You are good, that I am Yours, and that Your faithfulness will continue forever into the future.

NOTES

1. Charles Spurgeon, *Morning and Evening: Daily Readings*, Morning, September 25, on *Christian Classics Ethereal Library*, http://www.ccel.org/ccel/spurgeon/morneve.d0925am.html.

2. Phillip Keller, *A Shepherd Looks at Psalm 23* (Grand Rapids: Zondervan, 1970), 21.

3. Donald Miller, *Blue Like Jazz* (Nashville: Nelson, 2003), 14.

4. Austin Gutwein, *Take Your Best Shot: Do Something Bigger Than Yourself* (Nashville: Nelson, 2009), 67–68.

5. Sarah Young, *Jesus Calling: Enjoying Peace in His Presence* (Nashville: Nelson, 2004), 43.

6. "Rebecca St. James," *Forefront Records*, accessed November 5, 2010, http://rebeccastjames.forefrontrecords.com/biography/.

7. "Eagle's Strength," *Roy DeLaGarza Ministries*, accessed October 27, 2010, http://www.roydelagarza.com/id92.html.

8. Joshua Harris, *Dug Down Deep: Unearthing What I Believe and Why It Matters* (Colorado Springs: Multnomah, 2010), 63.

9. Angela Thomas, *A Beautiful Offering: Returning God's Love with Your Life* (Nashville: Nelson, 2004), 160–161.

10. David Jeremiah, *Turning Points: Moments of Decision in the Presence of God* (Brentwood, TN: Integrity, 2005), 242.

11. Max Lucado, *In the Grip of Grace* (Dallas: Word, 1996), 148.

12. Joni Eareckson Tada and Steven Estes, *When God Weeps: Why Our Sufferings Matter to the Almighty* (Grand Rapids: Zondervan, 1997), 124–125.

13. Sheila Walsh, *Extraordinary Faith* (Nashville: Nelson, 2005), 186.

14. Ken Boa and Larry Moody, *I'm Glad You Asked* (Colorado Springs: Cook Communications Ministries, 1982, 1994), 91.

15. Pete Wilson, *Plan B: What Do You Do When God Doesn't Show Up the Way You Thought He Would?* (Nashville: Nelson, 2010), 117.

16. Walsh, *Extraordinary Faith*, 50.

17. Matthew West, "Lessons Learned from a Lousy Day," *Matthew West* (blog), October 13, 2010, http://www.matthewwest.com/2010/10/13/lessons-learned-from-a-lousy-day/.

18. Angela Elwell Hunt, *Women of Faith Devotional Bible: A Message of Grace & Hope for Every Day* (Nashville: Nelson, 2010), 1519.

19. *Nelson's NKJV Study Bible* (Nashville: Nelson, 2005), 743.

20. John MacArthur, ed., *The MacArthur Study Bible* (Nashville: Nelson, 1997), 1805.

21. Alex and Brett Harris, *Do Hard Things: A Teenage Rebellion Against Low Expectations* (Colorado Springs: Multnomah, 2008), 4.

22. *The Rebelution*, accessed October 29, 2010, http://www.therebelution.com/books/.

23. "The Temperature of the World," *The Creation of the Universe*, accessed November 5, 2010, http://www.creationofuniverse.com/html/blue_planet_02.html.

24. Jenna Lucado, *Redefining Beautiful* (Nashville: Nelson, 2009), 39.

25. Young, *Jesus Calling*, 23.

26. Andy Stanley, *The Grace of God* (Nashville: Nelson, 2010), 104–105.

27. MacArthur, *The MacArthur Study Bible*, 1771.

28. Miller, *Blue Like Jazz*, 100.

29. Walsh, *Extraordinary Faith*, 59.

30. Wilson, *Plan B*, 35–36.

31. Paula Rinehart, *Women of Faith Devotional Bible*, 1541.

32. Miller, *Blue Like Jazz*, 173.

33. *Nelson's NKJV Study Bible*, 833.

34. Stormie Omartian, *The Power of a Praying Parent* (Eugene, OR: Harvest House, 1995), 18.

35. "What If Brother Lawrence Had a Dishwasher?" *Just Words* (blog), April 30, 2010, http://edsundaywinters.wordpress.com/2010/04/30/what-if-brother-lawrence-had-a-dishwasher/.

36. Lisa Whelchel, *Friendship for Grown-Ups: What I Missed & Learned Along the Way* (Nashville: Nelson, 2010), 135.

37. MacArthur, *The MacArthur Study Bible*, 1998.

38. *Nelson's NKJV Study Bible*, 1805.

39. Peter De Vries, *World of Quotes.com*, accessed November 14, 2010, http://www.worldofquotes.com/topic/Confession/index.html.

40. Jeremiah, *Turning Points*, 242.

41. Anne Jackson, *Permission to Speak Freely: Essays and Art on Fear, Confession, and Grace* (Nashville: Nelson, 2010), 118–119.

42. Natalie Grant, *The Real Me: Being the Girl God Sees* (Nashville: Nelson, 2005), 136–137.

43. *Women of Faith Devotional Bible*, 1519.

44. Kevin Davis, "'Greatness of Our God' by Natalie Grant," August 17, 2010, *New Release Tuesday.com*, http://www.newreleasetuesday.com/article.php?article_id=408.

45. Beth Moore, *To Live Is Christ: Embracing the Passion of Paul* (Nashville: Broadman & Holman, 2001), 272.

ACKNOWLEDGMENTS

We gratefully acknowledge the following authors and publishers for use of their material.

Ken Boa and Larry Moody. Excerpt from *I'm Glad You Asked*, ©1982 by Ken Boa and Larry Moody, published by David C. Cook. Publisher permission required to reproduce. All rights reserved.

Joni Eareckson Tada and Steven Estes. Excerpt from *When God Weeps*, ©1997 by Joni Eareckson Tada and Steven Estes. Reprinted by permission.

Natalie Grant. Excerpt from *The Real Me*, ©2005, Thomas Nelson Inc. Nashville, Tennessee. Reprinted by permission.

Austin Gutwein. Excerpt from *Take Your Best Shot*, ©2009, Thomas Nelson Inc. Nashville, Tennessee. Reprinted by permission.

Alex and Brett Harris. Excerpt from *Do Hard Things*, ©2008 by Alex and Brett Harris. Reprinted by permission.

Joshua Harris. Excerpt from *Dug Down Deep*, ©2010 by Joshua Harris. Reprinted by permission.

Anne Jackson. Excerpt from *Permission to Speak Freely*, ©2010, Thomas Nelson Inc. Nashville, Tennessee. Reprinted by permission.

David Jeremiah. Excerpt from *Turning Points*, ©2005, Thomas Nelson Inc. Nashville, Tennessee. Reprinted by permission.

Phillip Keller. Excerpt from *A Shepherd Looks at Psalm 23*, ©1970 by Phillip Keller. Reprinted by permission.

Jenna Lucado. Excerpt from *Redefining Beautiful*, ©2009, Thomas Nelson Inc. Nashville, Tennessee. Reprinted by permission.

Max Lucado. Excerpt from *In the Grip of Grace*, ©1996, Thomas Nelson Inc. Nashville, Tennessee. Reprinted by permission.

John MacArthur. Excerpt from *The MacArthur Study Bible*, edited by John MacArthur, ©1997, Thomas Nelson Inc. Nashville, Tennessee. Reprinted by permission.

Donald Miller. Excerpt from *Blue Like Jazz*, ©2003, Thomas Nelson Inc. Nashville, Tennessee. Reprinted by permission.

Beth Moore. Used by permission. Excerpt taken from *To Live Is Christ* by Beth Moore, ©2001 B & H Publishing Group.

Nelson's NKJV Study Bible. ©2005, Thomas Nelson Inc. Nashville, Tennessee. Reprinted by permission.

Stormie Omartian. Excerpt taken from *The Power of a Praying® Parent*, copyright ©1995/2005 by Stormie Omartian, Eugene, Oregon 97402, www.harvesthousepublishers.com. Used by permission.

Charles Spurgeon. Excerpt from *Morning and Evening: Daily Readings* by Charles Spurgeon, courtesy Christian Classics Ethereal Library.

Andy Stanley. Excerpt from *The Grace of God*, ©2010, Thomas Nelson Inc. Nashville, Tennessee. Reprinted by permission.

Angela Thomas. Excerpt from *A Beautiful Offering*, ©2004, Thomas Nelson Inc. Nashville, Tennessee. Reprinted by permission.

Sheila Walsh. Excerpt from *Extraordinary Faith*, ©2005, Thomas Nelson Inc. Nashville, Tennessee. Reprinted by permission.

Lisa Whelchel. Excerpt from *Friendship for Grown-Ups*, ©2010, Thomas Nelson Inc. Nashville, Tennessee. Reprinted by permission.

Pete Wilson. Excerpt from *Plan B*, ©2010, Thomas Nelson Inc. Nashville, Tennessee. Reprinted by permission.

Sarah Young. Excerpt from *Jesus Calling*, ©2004, Thomas Nelson Inc. Nashville, Tennessee. Reprinted by permission.

MY FAVORITE BIBLE VERSES

MY FAVORITE BIBLE VERSES

MY FAVORITE BIBLE VERSES